Fatima
At the Heart of the C

God's vision of history and ob

GW01087063

Fr Serafino M. Lanzetta

Fatima
At the Heart of the Church

God's vision of history and oblative spirituality

Tibi Virgo Sacrata
Ut Triumphum Immaculati Cordis Tui adveniat
XIII-V-MMXVIII

Contents

PART THREE

THE MESSAGE OF FATIMA IN THE LIGHT OF THE GOSPEL

PART FOUR
THE SECRET NOT YET REVEALED

Acknowledgments

This book on Fatima is published just one year after the great Centenary of Our Lady's apparitions at the Cova da Iria (1917-2017. One can definitely say that Fatima is contemporary and today more than ever shows its relevance as a great prophecy for the Church and the world. I'm glad that this book, after not a few hardships, comes out for the English readers. For this publication, I'm grateful to Liam Kelly for the translation from the original Italian, published by Casa Mariana Editrice 2017 (*Fatima un appello al cuore della Chiesa. Teologia della storia e spiritualità oblativa*). I have also to thank my confrere, Fr George M. Roth together with our parish secretary, Jacob Campbell, for proofreading the whole manuscript and making valuable suggestions. A thank you to Doug Savage too who helped me very much with his precious advises to make some important improvements. May Our Lady of Fatima reward them all. A special thought, while publishing this English edition, for all my parishioners of St Mary, Gosport (England), to whom I wish to dedicate in particular this work, with the prayer that they may come to know more deeply the beauty of the Fatima Message and its call to a profound love to the Immaculate Heart of Mary. From this key-point, the call to penance, sacrifice and prayer of the Holy Rosary takes vivid shape.

Introduction to the mystery of Fatima

For an appropriate understanding of the heavenly Message

Fatima: a theology of history

The Fatima-event marked the start of a path of renewal for the whole of the Church: the Lady dressed in White, who came from Heaven to speak to us through the three humble shepherd children, repeated to the 20th century and to today's humanity the eternal truth of the Gospel, but with a specific characteristic, identifying with it in history. The supernatural events – recognised as such by the approval of the Church – confirmed the historic facts and history was read by the Virgin herself in the light of God. Fatima tells us that history belongs to God and only in His light can we read its events, as threat or promise: that depends on us, if we leave room for the Gospel, the Word of God descended in time and in history.

Reflecting on the prodigious events which took place at Fatima in the distant year of 1917, from May to October, and prepared two years previously by the apparitions of the Angel, we notice a very interesting prior element, on which we must pause: God is the Lord of history, He guides it, events unfold with His permission towards a salvific goal and are not immutably pre-determined events, prisoners of anonymous forces of evil. So if God is the Lord of history, then love and freedom guide us, not fate and destiny. This also means that history is not already written to the detriment of the freedom of God and humanity, it can, instead, change, it can return to the source of truth if the human person changes inside drawing closer to God, if the human person leaves sin behind and converts.

Fatima tells us that history can change, must change, that history is the result of the freedom of people over which rules God's Providence, with a look of love imbued with justice and mercy. History is guided by God, but is placed into the hands of humankind, is consigned to the freedom of the human person which, however, cannot be total whim, it has a limit, and this limit is the Providence of love which rules everything and leads everything to a good end. At times this escapes us precisely because the God-Love loves to conceal Himself behind events, even the most perilous, loves the eloquent silence of daily events, of simple things, hides also in grief and suffering. In fact it is precisely here that at times He speaks in a stronger way and shakes us.

Fatima tells us that history can change if we change, if we pray. If we listen to Our Lady and do what She asked, then the course of our history can change, changing our being. Fatima tells us there are two weapons for bringing about a true revolution of history and in history: *prayer* and *penance*. With these the revolution is long-lasting, it inserts itself into the lowliest labyrinths of social structures, it innervates in secret where everything moves, everything works, where the most destructive as well as the greatest and most beneficial ideas are planned, in the secret where no ideologist can enter but only God and the human person: conscience and freedom.

If we pray our hearts change and we place our history, the history of humanity, into the lap of divine Providence. For its part, Providence enters into our world, enters us, and changes us. Prayer is an opening to God and God opens Himself to us, enters into us. We speak with the word of God and He speaks His words in us. He is in us and we are in Him. In the light of His words we can speak goodness and truth. Prayer teaches us to speak with the words of God and speak to humanity about the things of God, things eternal. What is eternal is true and prayer makes us speak of what is eternal. Only if we speak with God can we speak with humankind and say things that are true.

Every ideology pretends to speak to humankind about human things, but forgets that the human person who only speaks with him or herself soon becomes a threat to him or herself and to others; human affairs, too, soon become inhuman and in the name of ideas the living, men and women in flesh and blood, are crushed. The 20th century is a great lesson in inhumanity perpetrated in the name of humanity. At the start of that century, in Fatima, Our Lady reminded us that it is necessary to speak with God, to pray unceasingly with a prayer, the Holy Rosary, which is unceasing praise and constant request for mercy and salvation from eternal perdition. The person who does not speak with God loses the meaning of words, no longer knows what is truly good and starts to fall into lies. Those people who do not speak to God are to be feared!

The other great antidote to evil and to the damnation of history and humanity is penance. Through penance we make up for the evil done to God and to humanity, we purify ourselves and history from the snares and filth of evil. Interiorly renewed, we prepare ourselves to welcome the future as God's time for us, as a favourable time for humankind. Yes, penance does ensure Justice reconciles the world with God, the world with good, purifying evil, crushing its strength. Evil is not wiped out with a clean slate. It remains in the furrows carved out in our lives and in our history. It is utopian to think that evil is self-redeeming, that sooner or later it disappears, without a serious commitment to eradicate it through penance. God-less ideologies think that evil is only an error of history, when an implacable force looms over us and crushes us. In both cases the human person sees him or herself defenceless when faced with it: either he or she justifies it as good or just denounces it. Meanwhile, however, it remains and continues to demean. Its justification is false. Protest against God is false. Contempt for God due to evil is inhuman. That way humanity simply condemns itself and continues to live in the inferno of evil, but does not act. Just looks.

Fatima, instead, invites us to act, to do something to destroy evil and make human the face of humanity and of the world. It is necessary to fight sin, the root of all evil. It is necessary to redeem sin as offence against God and disdain for the things which God has created.

There is only one way, therefore, to overcome evil: redeem it, purify it. Through penance its power is destroyed and the world is opened to God. Penance thus opens us to reconciliation with God and with our brothers and sisters. While evil profoundly marks the human person, penance redeems the person, healing his or her wounds. In fact, the Good Samaritan, Jesus, bent over us to heal our wounds Himself.

Prayer and penance enable God to enter into history once again, they unite us to His will and so finally we know what is good, when one is living well, how to live well. This is not just for us, like selfish satisfaction, but always for everyone.

Fatima offers us a splendid theological vision of history and tells us: only with God can humanity continue to live. Only if we live for God does the world also live. To banish God from the world and from the heart of humanity leads to self-destruction: not just war, but the flaming sword of our soaring technology looms ready to destroy us.

Fatima: the truth about sin

At a time when already that culture of the absence of sin, which sadly would later be all the rage or see its justification as irrelevant, was beginning to take shape, Our Lady came to Fatima to tell us about the truth of this evil. It is a real and not theoretical evil as it might seem, simply because I can't touch it, I don't see it. Sin is truly an evil, it is the root of evil. Our Lady of Fatima comes to speak to us about the misery of sin and repeatedly tells us that God is very offended by the sins of humankind.

The daily temptation is always to blame others, to say that it is always others who are the cause of evil and therefore sin is always and only by others, in fact, other people are the real sin. In a deeply selfish world, the only sin is the limit to my free will. This limit comes from outside, either from God or from the human person. And so one does all one can to get rid of both God and humankind. That is why life is no longer relevant. I am the iniquitous arbiter of my life and so I condemn others to death, too. Unfortunately, you cannot see that there is a more intimate evil, more profound than my selfishness, which hides itself right in the tangle of my individualism and is called sin. Sin is contempt of God and consequently a selfish drawing in on oneself, a blind attack on the things that God has made.

Saint Thomas Aquinas gives the following definition of sin: "*Aversio a Deo et conversio ad creaturas* [a turning away from God and a turning towards earthly goods]". But this retreating to created things, to humankind, is it ultimately an advantage or, instead, a loss, ruin? Every sin is vanity if I disdain God, ultimately I have contempt also for the things I abuse, because I appropriate them separating them from their source, I manipulate them, I subjugate them to my whims. When God is no longer part of my life, things are no longer part of it either.

In the end, sin as an offence against God is real contempt for the world, creation, for things. If I have contempt for God and His Law I have contempt for everything that God has done. An offence against God is consequently an offence against all God has done, an insult to everything, the loss of everything. Mortal sin is the true loss of everything, of God and of things which are of God. There is not a "chance" creator and guardian of things, there is no fate which guards me in the absence of God. My life is already in the depths. For this reason, sin which remains in the human person can be embraced only by the eternal inferno: definitive perdition, the loss of God and things without God.

Fatima teaches us that evil is not banal, that sin is not an irrelevant phenomenon. In fact, it is a threat to the human person who offends God. Sin can even be the human person's definitive punishment, his or her loss.

To sin against God, to offend this Father of love by denying His will, is a real failure in life. To reject love and therefore true freedom to choose the condition of a servant, someone who no longer wants to sit at table with his or her Father, does not just offend God, but is a failure as a human person. The person who sins against God threatens him or herself and is heading towards ruin. That creation which isolates itself having excluded the Creator, sooner or later will appeal to human kind without its God. Creation becomes a threat to humanity, the very work of human hands becomes a trap for the freedom of humanity. The more humankind offends God, the more the world becomes a threat to humanity, its death sentence. Is it perhaps not true that the new and until recently totally unthinkable horizons reached by scientific progress are like a flaming sword hanging over the head of humanity? It follows humanity as it seeks new frontiers: if God and the moral principles of the truth of humanity are set aside, the new discoveries become death. Suffice to press a button at some nuclear centres to set fire to the whole of humanity in a few seconds. Suffice to cry out in the name of freedom of research in experimentation in order to exterminate a great number of frozen embryos: cellulose masses to be disposed – it is said – while in truth it is the dawning of real human lives. The more science distances itself from God, from truth, the more it becomes a flaming sword which strikes its heroes – men and women – and the innocent, especially the innocent.

The human person is a being in relation with God; if this relationship is excluded in the name of his or her freedom – the person can also do this precisely because they are free – they sin, or rather, die; even though he or she continues to live, the soul is dead, freedom is blind, it becomes free will and, sadly, it becomes death for others, too. To reject God, to deny Him, is really a disaster. Sin is humanity's real tragedy. Nothing will have a sense of sin. So it is no exaggeration to say that sin destroys the human person and the things of life; it orients them to selfishness, to self-sufficiency, to die in one's own misery. To the person who chooses sin there remains only their own self-commiseration, their own desperation: only with him or herself, abandoned by his or her "things", too. Creation accuses the evil human person before God. The wages of sin are really death.

As is said today, if sin is insignificant, why is evil spreading in such a frightful way? Is it because humanity gives death to humanity and in an increasingly "human" way? The genetic industry – in too many cases real eugenics – is today so "scientific" that it makes us proud to discard so many human lives from the outset, because they do not respond to the increasingly complex parameters of human health. Killing takes place in the name of health. Life is desired and death is provided. Why does nothingness cloak the lives of so many with no more meaning, with no more God?

Fatima warns us: sin is the true evil of the world and of humanity. Only true conversion, which is return to God through the renunciation of evil and sin, saves us, makes us truly human and opens before us the path to eternity, to love and to joy. To return to God is also to rediscover the things of life.

Fatima: the true evil of sin

At Fatima, the Lady dressed in White came to remind us of the drama of sin which perturbs humanity and indicates a destiny of suffering for peoples. Coming down into the history of that 20th century so cruelly tormented by nihilistic ideologies and by two World Wars which marked a true destruction, the Message of Fatima represents, at the same time, a warning and an appeal.

A warning so that men and women face the responsibility of their freedom abused in sin and an appeal to conversion to remedy evil, personal and social destruction.

In the distant July 1917, Sister Lucia recounts in her third *Memoir* the prophetic words of Our Lady after the vision of hell:

> *"You have seen hell where the souls of poor sinners go. To save them, God wishes to establish in the world devotion to my Immaculate Heart. If what I say to you is done, many souls will be saved and there will be peace. The war is going to end; but if people do not cease offending God, a worse one will break out during the pontificate of Pius XI".*

The cause of the war is the personal sin of the person who offends God and infringes His Law, which is quickly transformed into the social sin of people who become absolute arbiters of their own blind destiny. Sin is not an illusion, an invention by the Church to shake indolent souls, instead it is the verification of the disasters perpetrated by humanity itself which forgets God. Sin makes hatred and evil run through the veins of the world and humanity. As an offence against God, truth and goodness, it scatters lies, deceit between peoples. In sin, chosen as a paradigm of life, the very human person becomes a lie, a simple thing in the hands of the world, removed from his or her intrinsic truth as a creature. If the human person denies God, the world denies the human person who then finds him or herself alone only with themselves, alone in their evil against everyone.

Deep down, evil is not accidental. Sin is not marginal; instead it has eternal repercussions. Evil committed in time has echoes in eternity. Each time I act freely, in fact, I always choose the eternity of goodness. Since freedom stretches out towards the goodness which is right about infinity – good is endless because otherwise I would not be able to continue to choose it – from time to time freedom itself chooses the infinite. Even the choice of evil, which is a false good, an untrue good, provokes me in the choice of the infinite. Now, I can choose only between good and evil and not between eternity and time. In each of my choices I do not choose an evil or a good to enjoy for a time. Even if my choice is circumscribed by time, I do not want the time, I want that good until it is there, I want all the good I have chosen. I choose the eternity of the good or I can choose the eternity of the untrue good, hell.

Every good choice, therefore, be it true or false, is right about eternity. So, in every free action I always choose either Paradise or hell. I am faced with two paths every time: the path of life or the path of death.

Of course, this implies that sin is a real and not illusory evil, not – as gnostic and esoteric thought would have it – a good, a necessity for the dialectic cycle of affirmation accomplished by goodness through self-denial in its opposite. Sin in itself is always loss, emptiness, it can never become goodness, both because in itself it only has the reasoning of evil – evil is not a good – and because in its dialectic becoming true it is not goodness which follows but in any case and solely evil. The "friendly" encounter – so yearned for by the enlightened – between good and evil does not generate good but evil, a worse evil which waters down goodness in the vortex of nothingness and pain. For a while try to put together a good baby and a naughty uneducated baby. After a while, it usually happens that the good one learns the art of the bad one and the bad one grows in its corrupting malice. This is for the simple reason repeated by that wise saying which states: "*Bonum ex integra causa, malum ex quocumque defectu* [An action is good when good in every respect; it is wrong when wrong in any respect]". In fact, a drop of poison clouds a whole goatskin of wine.

And yet, we ask ourselves, faced with the horrific spectacle of evil – much more often, however, we hide from ourselves that this evil comes from the heart of the human person, from our intimate depths – : why is there evil in the world? Which is the same as saying: why is there not goodness in the world? Why is there not that goodness that I would like? I have been made for good, but I find evil. I would like good but I do evil. Why? These questions help us to understand that God is not the origin of evil, nor is there evil in God. I cannot simply unload the blame onto God and so absolve myself, I cannot accuse God of evil in the world, of my sin. It is rather a poisonous root which corrupts the will of humanity, the freedom of the human person. Sin is a real evil which worms its way into the human person and his or her choices, threatening them continually with falsehood and lies.

I cannot even get rid of sin by saying that deep down it is a mere transgression of a positive law written in the codex of God's Decalogue. Instead, it is rather breaking the Law of God written within us. Sin ruins what is in us, our intimate depths, our soul, ourselves. If we lose our soul we have truly lost everything. Sin strips us inwardly, wounds our being, making us less than we should be. It deprives us of the truth of being, therefore of goodness and love. The eternal loss, in other words the sin which remains, is the privation of the truth of being. Sin is always loss: it is renouncing what I should be.

Alas, sin has a price: failure, death, as closure to God, to truth and to love. The price of persistent sin is despair.

Our Lady appeared at Fatima precisely to give a remedy to the real evil of sin: She Herself, her Immaculate Heart. If we enter into Her Heart we are freed from evil. In Her Heart there is no place for sin, nor for the pride which is its root. If the whole Church were to enter into Her Immaculate Heart, the Immaculate Heart of Mary would triumph in the world. And so why not prepare in such a way for this victory?

Part One

The Angel's Apparitions

THE ANGELIC PREPARATION AT FATIMA

The three apparitions of the Angel preceded and prepared the apparitions of Our Lady, to help the little shepherd children to enter into the heart of the Message of Fatima which the Angel already set out along its essential lines. The little shepherds were themselves illiterate and Lucia herself, asked about the exact date of the Angel's apparitions, replied: "*I think it was in Spring 1916 that the Angel appeared to us for the first time*". Historical research has confirmed that the Angel's apparitions went on for about a year, between 1915 and 1916. We must bear in mind that they took place in the terrible context of the First World War, which had just broken out.

ANGELIC PRESENCE IN GOD'S PROVIDENTIAL PLAN

Before entering into the merits of the apparitions, it is useful to ask ourselves who are the angels and what is their role.

The presence of angels in *Sacred Scripture* is very clear. We refer to it because it is the foundation of our Faith, the first channel through which God's Revelation comes to us. The Bible reports divine manifestations so that through them humanity may know God.

The other foundation aimed at transmitting Revelation is *Tradition*, that is, the totality of the teachings of the Apostles, the Fathers of the Church and the Magisterium. It follows that all that does not fall within Sacred Scripture and Tradition is not the Revelation of God, which is defined as "public"; the apparitions of the Angel and the Message of Fatima are to be listed among the so-called "private" revelations, which the Church declares authentic only when in conformity with the public Revelation: the private message must never move away from the content of the Gospel and from God's way of working in Sacred Scripture; on a number of occasions we will notice the great inter-dependence between Revelation and the Message of Fatima.

Many episodes in Sacred Scripture attest repeatedly to the existence of these spiritual beings, sent by God to carry out a particular mission. The "angel" means literally "messenger", designating its mission and not its nature. This messenger is an angelic person, a spiritual being composed simply of spirit, of a spiritual nature from which spiritual activities begin; therefore, the angels are real creatures, persons capable of thinking, wanting, loving, choosing, remembering, communicating with thought: all qualities which determine a spiritual nature. The angel is created by God as a spiritual being, that is, without a body, and hence in the *Credo* mention is made of the creation of things visible and invisible. This reference to invisible things refers precisely to angels.

Unlike angels, humans are people composed of spirit and matter, whose spiritual activities are manifested in the body. In this mediation of the body there exists the possibility of the perfection of our spiritual activities decreasing, while the angel enjoys a perfect nature, because it is not bound to this imperfection which is the body. So the angel draws closer to the human person than to the perfection of God and therefore is an intermediary between God and humankind, with the role of mediating between the two: transmitting God's messages to humanity to help humanity draw closer to God. If there were no angels, the human person would not have the capacity to form a relationship with God and would easily fall into polytheist adoration, since humanity would think that all forces superior to it were attributable to divinities. Ancient mythology did nothing but worship the natural forces superior to humankind – like the force of the storm, or the sea – assigning a divinity to each; this error was possible because, deep down, angels were not thought of nor believed in. All that is superior to the human person but inferior to God is attributable to the activity of the angelic creatures which we know can be both good and evil: there are angels and demons, the former serve God, the latter at the service of evil and of Satan.

The angels carry out an important role both on the level of creation and of our spiritual life: they are creatures whom God has put in our path so that they might lead us always to Him. If we think of the Guardian Angel who accompanies us on the earthly journey to help us also in those things that would be impossible to us humans: if we pray to the Angel with faith, he answers us. His is a spiritual but real presence. He can carry out many services, sometimes resolving even the most banal problems, like delaying the departure of a bus or a train, so that you don't lose your way, or find parking... Try it! But the Angel wants to be invoked above all to help us get to Paradise.

THE ANGEL OF FATIMA: PREPARATORY MISSION

What has been said helps us to understand that the Angel of Fatima had the role of helping the three little shepherd children to prepare themselves for the coming of Our Lady and already this makes us reflect on the unity between Fatima and public Revelation. Carefully observing the content of the apparitions, one notices a very strong resemblance between the Angel of Fatima and the Angel of Yahweh. Suffice to recall that Abraham, at the oaks of Mamre, had a manifestation of God Himself who announced to Sarah the imminent conception, despite her old age (cf. *Gen* 18:1-16. The Fathers of the Church saw in this apparition of the Angel of Yahweh, through human figures, a first manifestation of the mystery of the Most Holy Trinity. This means that the Angel of light is always he who manifests God and brings God's message to humanity. Just as the Angel who informed Samson's mother that she would soon conceive and give birth to a son who would be a Nazarite, that is, consecrated to God (cf. *Judg* 13:3-6); or the Angel who announced to Mary Most Holy the imminent conception of a Son, who would be the Holy One of God (cf. *Lk* 1:26-28).

The Angel of Fatima sent by God to bring an introductory announcement to the message of Our Lady already outlines the nucleus of the Message of Fatima: worship God, recognised as the Most Holy Trinity, and make reparation for the sins of humanity. There is great similarity with the apparition at the oaks of Mamre: the Angel prepared Abraham for the mystery of the Most Holy Trinity, while at Fatima the Angel taught the three little shepherds a prayer of adoration of the Trinity: "*My God, I believe, I adore, I hope and I love You! I ask pardon of You for those who do not believe, do not adore, do not hope and do not love You*", which is preparation for the Trinitarian prayer of the third apparition:

> "*Most Holy Trinity, Father, Son and Holy Spirit, I offer You the most precious Body, Blood, Soul and Divinity of Jesus Christ, present in all the tabernacles of the world, in reparation for the outrages, sacrileges and indifference with which He Himself is offended. And through the infinite merits of His most sacred Heart, and the Immaculate Heart of Mary, I beg of You the conversion of poor sinners*".

The Angel brought the proclamation of the truth of God, One and Three, who must be adored, inviting adoration to be followed by reparation for sins committed against God, against His holiness. Here, too, the Angel, messenger of God, is the one who indicates God, and such similarity between the Message of Fatima and Sacred Scripture is important, because it led the Church to pronounce on the veracity of these apparitions.

Another point of affinity with Sacred Scripture lies in the fact that the angelic reality of the messenger is not immediately grasped, but only after having reflected on the message given and having noted its majesty and beauty. This is what happened at Fatima: initially the children were frightened at the Angel's apparition; then it was the same mysterious figure who invited them not to be frightened, confirming having come from God. Only then was it understood that the figure was an Angel.

First apparition: the "Angel of Peace"

In the first apparition in 1915, the angelic creature presented himself as the "Angel of peace". The children were playing at Cabeço, while the sheep were grazing, when they became aware of a young man between 14 and 15 years old, whiter than snow, of extraordinary beauty. It was the Angel who presented himself: *"Do not be afraid! I am the Angel of Peace. Pray with me"*. The divine majesty with which the Angel of light was covered is a messenger of peace; what comes from God is always accompanied by the gift of peace. What needs to be underlined most of all is the appeal of the Angel of Peace: *"Pray with me"*. It is a very important invitation, especially nowadays, when there is so much talk of peace, but unfortunately with a mistaken idea of it, just as it was mistaken to define as a "symbol of peace" that banner with a coloured rainbow, reversed in order, which in fact represents the individual who, no longer recognising him or herself as a creature, rebels against every order and fights against God, cause of his or her "imprisonment". Peace is proclaimed, but without order and truth there is a continuous war even if weapons at first glance are silent. There is no desire to understand that peace is a gift from God, that it is not something achieved by marches and flags, but by prayer which re-establishes the order of the creature with his or her Creator.

A catechesis on prayer

The attitude of the Angel, who bows in a position of prostration, repeating three times the prayer which we will look at further on, has a pedagogical function: that of teaching children how to pray correctly and that the external attitude is important in prayer; in fact, the little shepherd children would imitate the Angel's position, prostrating themselves for a long time in a prayer rich in sacrifice. The Angel teaches us about the truths of God and, kneeling down, bows until his forehead touches the ground, in a real and proper prostration, to teach us the prayer of adoration of God. By this gesture he teaches that prayer must be accompanied by a correct attitude of the body, which must concentrate with the spirit, otherwise one does not pray correctly, one ends up thinking about everything except the words which are uttered. When one prays, the body must concentrate and assume an attitude of adoration towards God.

It often happens that people pray immediately after a completely different activity, even after having watched television. Clearly the body, at the time of prayer, is still in front of the television or immersed in the occupation just ended. To pray, the body must follow the spirit, because the human person is a profound unity of body and spirit and our spiritual actions always manifest themselves through the mediation of the body. Prayer, which is the greatest spiritual activity, is always mediated by our body: if the body is listless and lazy, our prayer, too, will be distracted. So the body must be focused and concentrated with the soul; it is as important as the soul for fruitful prayer.

To give an example, to have your legs crossed during prayer is a relaxed position which causes distraction, because it is an attitude which indicates on one hand the desire to rest, and on the other to pray: it is impossible to reconcile the two. The body must assume a position of prayer and the more the attitude is composed, attentive, devout, the more the soul is concentrated and avoids distraction.

Padre Pio of Pietrelcina always prayed with his hands on his forehead, because, by covering his face, he entered more easily into the mystery of God; Saint Francis of Assisi loved to pray closing himself into "the cell of his body", covering his head with his hood to encourage reflection: thus he made of his body a retreat where he knew he could gather in prayer. This is the characteristic proper to Christian prayer: the body must become a cell one enters to unite oneself to the mystery of God.

The three theological virtues – faith, hope and charity – closely linked, are at the basis of our spiritual life. Prostrating himself, the Angel taught this prayer, in which there is no specific reference to the Trinity of God, because it is an introductory prayer:

> *"My God, I believe, I adore, I hope and I love You! I ask pardon of You for those who do not believe, do not adore, do not hope and do not love You".*

It is an urgent invitation for us who listen to the Message of Fatima, which consists in adoring the mystery of God, hoping in what God has promised us and loving Him and one's brothers and sisters, especially poor sinners, imploring their salvation.

In fact it was not with the intention of frightening them that Our Lady revealed hell to the little shepherd children, as we will see, but to encourage them to generosity in reparative sacrifices, which avoid the eternal ruin of sinners. First the Angel taught the profession of Faith, adoration and hope and, immediately afterwards, called for reparation.

The nucleus of the Message of Fatima is prayer, adoration and reparation: we are called to adore God and make reparation for all the sins of those who do not adore Him and do not love Him. This Message is very topical for today's world increasingly distant from God and unaware that this separation is the ruin of humanity, is fatal. The little shepherd children were chosen to bring to the world a message of salvation, the only salvation possible.

Adoration and reparation

Rising, the Angel said: "*Pray thus. The Hearts of Jesus and Mary are attentive to the voice of your supplications*", inviting them to that prayer of adoration and reparation. The term "adoration" derives from the Latin "*adoratio*" (*ad-oratio*, "*ad-os*", where "*os*" is mouth; it is highly likely it comes from "*manus ad os mittere*": to bring one's hands to one's mouth) and recalls the action of bringing one's joined hands to one's lips – in pagan worship it meant kissing the hand of the god one wanted to honour – to the One who loved us to the point of kissing us in His Incarnation, as the Fathers of the Church said. Using a figurative action, to adore means to kiss God Himself and to allow oneself to be kissed by Him. Just as a kiss is a sign of affection, of love, so adoration is humanity's turning to God with a kiss to remain in His love.

It is God Himself who asks our *ad-oration*, a dialogue with the lips, but not chit-chat: a conversation which must be an immersion in the mystery of God. I adore because my whole life stretches towards God; as a consequence I must beg forgiveness for those who reject God, who will end up adoring themselves, since the human person cannot help but worship. Mind you that self-adoration, as we read in the temptation of Jesus in the desert, is always adoration of the prince of this world: the demon is satisfied and invites us to adore ourselves, as long as we do not worship God; but behaving thus, we carry out the will of Satan, we make ourselves his adorers.

So we can understand the Angel's request to pray and ask forgiveness for those who do not adore God, because this attitude is a symptom of perdition. We cannot thank God for our Faith and be resigned about the apostasy of others, believing that atheists, too, will be able to save themselves, according to the thought of Karl Rahner, for whom every creature has in themselves a sense of God even though not always thematic or objective, even when they deny Him, while God, for His part, would already be present in every human person precisely because they are a human person, thus blending nature and grace. This is absolutely false. God is not the fruit of our perception and moreover resides only in the heart in grace, free from sin.

Thus can be understood the Angel's request to adore and make reparation for the rejection of God: a most grave sin which prevents salvation. Adoring and making reparation, we implore from God pardon for sinners and therefore we beg their salvation. We must not forget that the Angel gives to each of us this mission: to speak about Jesus by our lives and our hearts, on behalf of those who prefer to adore the prince of this world; to kiss Jesus for those who spit on him.

Second apparition: the "Angel of Portugal"

In the first apparition the Angel had said: "*The Hearts of Jesus and Mary are attentive to the voice of your supplications*". He will repeat the same idea in the second apparition: "*The most holy Hearts of Jesus and Mary have designs of mercy on you*". Note how the heavenly Messenger speaks again about the Hearts of Jesus and Mary as one Heart, indissolubly linked: Mother and Son united in a redemptive covenant.

Such a great and demanding message is given to the three children, who were moreover illiterate. In effect, it was all those little ones could do: adoration and penance, the most necessary things, the medicines which obtain salvation. But it is also true that the Kingdom of heaven belongs to children (*Matt* 19:14 and whoever does not become like a little child will not enter the Kingdom of heaven (cf. *Matt* 18:3. The Angel and Our Lady speak to the children precisely because they are pure of heart and welcome in their simplicity the Message for what it is, without changing it or interpreting it. If the Immaculate had appeared to any excessive theologian, without a doubt they would have reported the opposite of what She was asking and with their intelligence and knowledge would have put in the mouth of Our Lady completely different words, would have thought of doing a good hermeneutic of it!

We, too, must imitate the three little shepherd children in the attitude of simple acceptance of the Message of Fatima, if we want to understand it; if, on the other hand, we prefer to interpret the words of Our Lady with our pride, we will end up rejecting Her Message, rejecting as well the major teaching of the three little shepherd children: simplicity of heart, the key-message of the Gospel. If we do not become pure and simple like those children it is not possible to penetrate the message of salvation. The Angel and Our Lady ask us for adoration and sacrifice in order to make us small and pure like children.

It is beautiful to think that when we are in God's presence we will see Him under the appearance of a child and if we succeed in looking into His clear eyes, to bear that pure and simple look, then we will be admitted to His Kingdom, even if having had to purify all the dross of sins in Purgatory; otherwise, we will not be able to remain with Him in eternity. It is an interesting metaphor to understand that ultimately God is absolute simplicity and purity and for this made Himself a child.

However, sometimes we look at simplicity with suspicion, because we think that it is an accessory to pestering and abuse of power by others, confusing instead simplicity with naivety and triviality. In fact, it is a most significant and important virtue: it is an attribute of God's being. Simplicity means absence of composition, of superfluous things. In God there is no composition, because He is devoid of matter. In God there is no duality, but absolute simplicity.

So, if we want truly to be Christians, we must become like the little shepherd children of Fatima, given to us as models so that we might become like little children, too, like the Infant Jesus.

That is why Our Lady suggests this most noble Message to three poor little shepherd children, recalling the Gospel: to little ones is given the ability to understand the mysteries of the Kingdom (cf. *Lk* 10:21). This very close similarity with Revelation often returns.

Pray "without pause..."

Sister Lucia recalls vaguely the date of the second apparition: "Some time passed, and summer came", she writes in her Memoirs. That should not cause surprise because the illiterate little shepherd children did not know how to check the calendar; they didn't even know what year they were in and so subsequently only approximately could the span of time (1915-1916) which covered the Angel's three apparitions be determined. The children were also unaware of the sequence of months, hence Sister Lucia, when she wrote, was uncertain about the year, the month and the day: this explains the very imprecise annotation about the time of the apparition. She will remember the day and month of Our Lady's apparitions because they will always take place on the 13th.

It must have been a rather long time between the Angel's apparitions, because note that the children, after the first apparition, seemed to have forgotten the call to prayer and reparation, so much so that the Angel had to reprimand them while they were playing close to the well – something natural at their age – admonishing them as if they were adults:

> "*What are you doing? Pray, pray very much! The most holy Hearts of Jesus and Mary have designs of mercy on you. Offer prayers and sacrifices constantly to the Most High*".

These words remind us of Jesus' call to pray continuously, without ever tiring (cf. Lk 18:1-8), echoing that "Watch and pray" (Matt 26:41).

"Without pause", "at all times", "without ever tiring": these are expressions which indicate that the entire life of the Christian must be a continual prayer. This phrase of Saint Paul: "So, whether you eat or drink, or whatever you do, do everything for the glory of God" (1 Cor 10:31), helps in understanding what it means to pray always: our whole lives, all our activities and actions, all our thoughts, everything we are and do, everything must become a constant prayer, supplication, giving thanks to God; if everything is done in this spirit, everything becomes prayer and so we pray without ever getting tired. Even sleeping, if done in the spirit of rendering thanks to God, becomes prayer. To pray unceasingly does not mean just directing the whole of one's life towards giving thanks, but also choosing precise times of prayer when, besides the intention, I also add the action of prayer, without believing it is possible to avoid times of prayer simply because I have the general intention of transforming the whole of life into prayer.

In such case we will recognise as valid the affirmation of some Christians who believe that one heartfelt Hail Mary is worth more than a monotonous 50 Hail Marys. This is false, because each person is fulfilled through their actions, which are actions that are repeated; the more I repeat a good action the more I am educated in doing good, that is, I improve myself, while the evil action, oft-repeated, marks me as worse. It is not the same thing to eat once or twice, it is not sufficient to eat plenty thinking there will be no further need to eat. One cannot say to one's spouse: "I love" once and for all, never to say it again. Doubtless the spouse will expect to hear it repeated every day and the more it is said to him or her, the more he or she will believe in those words. To say it just once in life, perhaps at the moment of marriage, would indicate that something is not right: the more the spouse is reminded that he or she is loved, the more love will grow, but otherwise it would dry up to the point of dying.

The same happens in prayer. It is not the same to say the Hail Mary once or a hundred times: the more one turns to Our Lady, the more love for Her grows and the more one improves in the life of prayer, growing as Christians. Whoever says that one heartfelt Hail Mary is sufficient finds they are mediocre Christians, incapable of growing in the spiritual life. So to pray unceasingly means to have specific moments of prayer, when you pray. To pray unceasingly means, therefore, to pray as much as I can so as to transform my life into a prayer pleasing to God.

This helps us understand that the life of prayer is perfected through prayer: the more I pray, the more my life becomes prayer and so I fulfil Jesus' exhortation: "Pray without ceasing and never lose heart" (cf. Lk 18:1-8). That is why Saint Alphonsus Maria de' Liguori said that whoever prays saves themselves, whoever does not pray condemns themselves and whoever prays just a little endangers themselves, because prayer is the constant nourishment of the soul. For this same reason the Angel suggested: "Offer prayers and sacrifices constantly to the Most High".

...and make sacrifices

It is interesting to observe how the little shepherd children understood this exhortation literally: they would always be faithful to prayer, using every moment and opportunity to offer sacrifices, even remaining prostrate for hours in prayer of adoration, so much so that sometimes little Francisco was unable to sustain that position.

Lucia asked the Angel:

> "*How are we to make sacrifices?*", and the Angel answered: "*Make of everything you can a sacrifice, and offer it to God as an act of reparation for the sins by which He is offended, and in supplication for the conversion of sinners*".

27

This response must stimulate us, too, recalling the phrase of Saint Paul to Timothy: "Proclaim the message; be persistent whether the time is favourable or unfavourable" (2 Tim 4:2), in the sense that one always needs to be ready to act.

The Angel continues, now presenting himself as the guardian Angel of Portugal:

> "*You will thus draw down peace upon your country. I am its Angel Guardian, the Angel of Portugal. Above all, accept and bear with submission, the suffering which the Lord will send you*".

These are very strong words for the children. Some believe that it is a message which is anything but educational, referring above all to the vision of hell. According to these opinions, the little shepherd children would have just remained frightened by it, finding themselves faced with the (old) version of a God in contrast with the truth, that is, a God who exacts revenge and takes pleasure in suffering. It is to be wondered if such statements come from those who refuse to correspond with the Angel's requests!

This message can seem anti-educational, but Our Lady has chosen these three little ones precisely to guarantee the simplicity and prosperity of the message, to stop it being manipulated by human minds, by humanity's rationality, which often tries to turn things to its own advantage. What's more, the Holy Virgin only said what is already affirmed in the Gospel, whose authors were not four great literati, but the Holy Spirit who animated the Gospel with his life-giving breath.

The pedagogy of Fatima ultimately reveals the seriousness of this Message which comes from Heaven as a message of salvation: we are saved if we do what the Message asks, without any manipulation, just as there can be no salvation for us through the manipulation of the Gospel. In both cases it is essential to preserve authenticity. If humanly speaking this Message can seem even harmful, especially for infantile pedagogy, one must remember that in the Gospel, too, the crucifixion of God seems anti-educational: in fact, it is a cause of scandal for many who reject a scourged and crucified God. However, God confounds the logic of force with weakness and the foolishness of the Cross.

In the Message of Fatima it is the logic of God, rather than the logic of the world, which has value. So we are on the good path: that of the Gospel!

Third apparition: a compendium of theology

1916 saw the third and last apparition of the Angel, very beautiful, focussed on Eucharistic reparation. Sister Lucia recounts that while they were saying the Holy Rosary, they saw the Angel again, who was carrying in his hands a chalice and a Host from which fell drops of blood into the chalice beneath. The Angel left the chalice and Host suspended in the air, knelt down beside the little shepherd children and taught them a prayer of adoration and reparation, a continuation of that taught in the first apparition.

The content of the Message progresses because in the first prayer the Angel was speaking of God, while in this he speaks of the Trinity:

> *"Most Holy Trinity, Father, Son and Holy Spirit, I offer You the most precious Body, Blood, Soul and Divinity of Jesus Christ, present in all the tabernacles of the world, in reparation for the outrages, sacrileges and indifference with which He Himself is offended. And through the infinite merits of His most sacred Heart, and the Immaculate Heart of Mary, I beg of You the conversion of poor sinners".*

Again there emerges the covenant between the Hearts of Jesus and Mary and noticeable, too, is how very closely linked are adoration of God and reparation for offences against the Hearts of Jesus and Mary. Our Lady, in fact, will reveal to Lucia her Heart surrounded by thorns due to our sins.

This progress in the revelation of Fatima is the sign of a strong symbiosis with the Revelation of God, where there exists a real development and evolution: one starts from God who reveals Himself through Moses in the Old Testament, to reach God who reveals Himself definitively in the Incarnation of Jesus. As God accompanies the human person to recognise His truth, so the Angel – and this is the real pedagogy – leads the children of Fatima to understand the mystery of God, who is Trinity, at whose centre is Jesus, present in all the Tabernacles of the world.

Here one finds a strong analogy with the prayer of Saint Francis, reported in the *Fonti Francescane*:

> "*We adore you, most holy Lord Jesus Christ, here, and in all your churches throughout the world; and we bless you, because by your holy Cross you have redeemed the world*" (*Fonti Francescane*, n. III).

When the Saint of Assisi adored Eucharistic Jesus in a church, he was adoring Him also in all the Tabernacles of the world, especially in those most abandoned. The prayer of the Christian is always a universal prayer, because the Christian wants to adore Jesus, present in all those places where there is a consecrated Host, and this adoration is a aimed at making reparation for all the offences and sacrileges committed against the Body and Blood of Christ.

It can be said that this prayer taught by the Angel is a synthesis of the whole of Theology: there is the mystery of the Triune God and the Most Holy Eucharist, the Body, Blood, Soul and Divinity of Jesus, the whole of Jesus. The Son gives Himself to us, to all those who receive Him in this divine Sacrament, to the just as well as the wicked: it is a great mystery. Jesus is silent and does not draw back even when faced with a soul in a state of sin who goes to receive Him, because He gave Himself out of love. A love sacrificed *even to the end*.

The Angel asked the children, who were simple, capable of true adoration with heart and with their lives, to make reparation for such sacrileges, alas in our days evermore numerous due also to black Masses and all sorts of perversion with regard to the Eucharist. While on the one hand there is an atmosphere of great indifference towards the gift of the Eucharist, on the other hand hostility and impiety towards it is growing. We must all learn by heart this prayer of reparation taught by the Angel of Fatima, to repeat it often in an attitude of reparation for the sins committed against the Most Holy Eucharist.

Having taught this prayer, the Angel got up and took in his hands the chalice and Host and gave communion to the three little shepherd children, giving the Host to Lucia, and the Blood to Francisco and to Jacinta: "*Take and drink the Body and Blood of Jesus Christ, horribly outraged by ungrateful men! Make reparation for their crimes and console your God*", and prostrating himself on the ground again repeated the same prayer three times.

The words "*console your God*" made a strong impression above all on the soul of Francisco; the other two little shepherd children from that moment often saw him crossing himself, crying, praying and making sacrifices, and when they asked him the reason for his isolation, he replied: "*I prefer praying alone, to think and console the Lord who is so sad*".

In his simplicity as a child, he often repeated that God "*is sad because of so many sins*". It must be well understood that this expression does not refer to any upset in God: God's "sadness" is certainly not the sadness of humanity, rather it is an analogous way of speaking borrowed from human experience. However, it is true that sin, as an offence against God, is always an offence which does not leave the Lord indifferent. It is an insult to His holiness and is equivalent, in a certain way, to hitting one's own parents. So, to

31

understand the gravity of the blasphemy, suffice to think of the insult which would be caused to a father if you spat in his face.

To make reparation for the sins of the world, then, Francisco loved to go to church to adore "Jesus hidden"; other times Lucia glimpsed him praying on a great stone, completely intent on consoling his God.

In the next chapter we will focus at length on the figures of St Francisco and St Jacinta, from whom we can really learn so much. Suffice for now to consider this: following the example of the little shepherd children of Fatima, our prayer must be a prayer of adoration and reparation, with the aim of *consoling* God, becoming, that is, *co-redeemers* in the salvation of one's neighbour, making reparation for all the sins against God and especially against the Eucharist.

We will come back to these aspects so fundamental for the Christian life.

Part Two

The apparitions
of the Lady dressed in White

The Topicality of the Message of Fatima

In May 2010 the Holy Father Benedict XVI went on pilgrimage to Fatima, broadening further the spiritual horizons of the Message of Fatima. In fact, it was thought that with the revelation of the third part of the Secret – which happened in 2000 and concerned largely the 20th century – the prophecy of Fatima was now concluded. Instead, the Holy Father Benedict XVI stated that the message of Fatima was still an open message, a prophecy which must still be fully realised. Therefore we will seek to understand the greatness of this message which Our Lady entrusted to the very simple and illiterate three little shepherd children, a message which is reflected exactly in historical events, reads those events in the light of God and, above all, provides us with the key for living today in the light of God and of the Faith.

Our Lady of Fatima provides a remedy: asks for the consecration to Her Immaculate Heart as refuge for saving us and all souls from eternal death. Another very interesting and topical thing is that Fatima, in the message which Our Lady gave to the little shepherd children, is not afraid to state that the unwanted events of life, even the most terrible ones, such as war, are allowed by God as punishment for our sins. And if we do not convert, the tragedy will be terrible, definitive. This is the greatness of Fatima: to see all that has happened and what is happening not as something simply casual or part of human affairs; no, all that is happening is God's will, so that humanity might convert and hope in eternal salvation. At this point one realises how necessary is the intervention of grace; may Our Lady open our minds and our hearts so that each of us may be able to deepen, especially through personal prayer with the recitation of the Holy Rosary, the beauty of this message. From a certain point of view it is a terrible message, which speaks of war, of eternal perdition, of hell, of sins which offend the Immaculate Heart of Mary and pierce it with sharp thorns, of natural catastrophes, etc., but there is also an element of hope: the offer which Our Lady makes of Herself, the gift of a unique remedy, which is the consecration to Her Immaculate Heart.

Tragedy or hope? We must say both, in so far as we choose to side with God and the Immaculate or that of guilty indifference.

The most beautiful grace which we should ask in the approach to the heavenly message is that of understanding that the Christian life requires a more holy living, that is more in harmony with God's will: that is precisely the request of Our Lady of Fatima; it is not enough to be mediocre Christians content with Baptism, instead we must be Christians according to the Immaculate Heart of Mary. Fatima wants to renew everyone in the spiritual life, bestow that spiritual strength which enables us to live as authentic Christians, as Christians who must save themselves for ever and only thus save the world.

Unfortunately, these ideas are rarely heard now. One of the ideas which has fallen largely into disuse today in homilies, in conferences, in catechesis is precisely that of "eternal salvation" and with it also the eternal realities, the ultimate truths of our life have been forgotten. It seems that the whole of Christian life is determined in keeping calm, in love of self, and rejoicing, because "we have already arisen", already been saved, while in fact, in the midst of so much euphoria, it is nothing but a losing sight of what is the end of our life, the goal of our Faith, as Saint Peter says (cf. *1 Pet* 1:9): the salvation of souls. This salvation can only pass through death to sin and therefore re-birth with Jesus to the life of grace.

If we want to briefly summarise the Message of Fatima, we can say that it consists in dying to sin – which sadly leads many souls to eternal perdition, as Our Lady said to the little shepherds – to be re-born as children of God and to live in the grace of God's children.

THE WONDERS OF FATIMA

In this section we will try to outline the "wonders of Fatima", that prodigious message which Our Lady brought from Heaven and which is integrated so harmoniously in the life of the Church. It is a message which reflects the teaching of the Gospel and above all demonstrates its topicality. Our Lady teaches something fundamental: the Christian life is a call to eternal salvation, it is not something discretionary, optional; salvation is a decisive fact for the life of each individual, especially for the eternal Life to which we are called.

Fatima is a great prophecy of the 20th century which has not ended, in fact, right now when the Church is experiencing a crisis never known before and when we hope Our Lady's words may quickly come true about the victory of her Immaculate Heart, it becomes ever more present.

So, what is the prophecy of Fatima? What did Our Lady reveal at Fatima? Before entering into the merit of the apparitions, let us focus for a while on a fundamental distinction, already referred to in reference to the angelic preparation for the Fatima event.

Public revelation and private revelations

First of all, it is important to distinguish between a private revelation, like that of Fatima, and the Revelation par excellence which is that which establishes our Catholic Faith, the so-called "public" Revelation. They are two different things, but united and inter-dependent.

Our Catholic Faith is founded on the Revelation of God: God has manifested to humankind the supernatural truths; the human person believes and responds to God with faith. There are two sources of this Revelation: Sacred Scripture, that is all that is written in the divine Scriptures, and Sacred Tradition, that is the Church itself which receives these truths from God, which speaks and in turn guards them and hands them on. In giving them back to humanity from age to age, from century to century, the Church gives the divine Faith to the generations.

Therefore, our Faith, the Faith which obliges us, the Faith which saves us, is contained in this divine Revelation, whose centre is Christ, God made man, God who became flesh, suffered, died and rose: the Redemption of Christ as liberation from sin and eternal salvation from hell, from perdition. This is the public Revelation, which establishes our Faith; the unique Revelation necessary for the Faith.

The other revelations, those so-called "private" revelations, are not indispensable for Faith, but only when they are in harmony with this divine Revelation are they useful and necessary to deepen the Faith and all that the Gospel teaches. They are called "private" because they do not belong to the patrimony of the public Revelation and not because they are destined for subjective discernment.

Private revelations, because they are of help, must necessarily be in conformity with the one Revelation which constitutes the nucleus of our Faith. By private revelations are meant those supernatural manifestations or prophecies which come from God, from Heaven, from Our Lady, as help to understand better the Gospel and above all to contextualise it from time to time. Such supernatural manifestations, however, require a judgement of authentication from the Church, so that it may have the certainty that it is an authentic manifestation of the supernatural.

Why is it necessary that the Church express itself? Because the one Revelation necessary for our salvation was consigned by God to the Church. The Church is the guarantor, the deposit of this Revelation, which it guards most faithfully and hands on. Therefore the Church is the sole guarantor of the authenticity of a supernatural manifestation. By Church here we mean not the mystical Body as such but the sacred hierarchy, the Apostles, therefore their successors, that is, the bishops with the Pope as head.

The judgement of Holy Mother Church

In the procedure for the recognition of a supernatural event the first word belongs to the diocesan bishop. If, then, the event is important and goes beyond the diocesan or national boundaries, it is referred to the Holy See. This is what happened for Fatima.

There are three ways in which the Church can express a judgement on private revelations.

a) After a careful analysis of the supernatural manifestations, the messages and the historical evolution of these revelations, and having received a supernatural confirmation by a miracle, for which there must be clear, scientific proof, the Church expresses the following judgement: "*It consists of the supernatural*", that is, this message comes from God. The consequence is that the faithful can follow it without fear of deceit. Of course that message does not require the same faith by which we believe that Jesus Christ is the Son of God, made flesh and risen from the dead, but gives a moral guarantee that, following its teachings, one will receive supernatural help to save oneself. In other words, we are not obliged to believe in the Message as in the articles of Faith, but to reject it or even despise it would be rash and misleading.

b) Another type of judgement is when the Church affirms that the private revelation "*does not consist of the supernatural*". That means that from the examinations carried out the decisive reason for saying that God has really intervened in that context is not yet clear. However, it is not yet a definitive judgement. This is the case of Medjugorje: the current judgement of the Croatian Bishops' Conference maintains that up to now these private revelations do not consist of the supernatural. That is why anyone who goes to Medjugorje must go there not with the intention of seeing Our Lady or because Our Lady appears, but to undertake a simple pilgrimage of faith and prayer in a Marian shrine. However, there is the possibility that in the future – in an analysis at the end of these revelations which are still on-going – a different judgement may be reached. The current Bishop of Mostar, Rakto Perić, in fact, is highly sceptical: even in the very early days of the apparitions – which in the judgement of others would be the only true ones, while the ongoing ones would be affected and worsened by human interference – they were affected by things too human, all paving the way for deception. We hope that the universal Church, which has arrogated the investigation to itself, can provide a judgement of the Medjugorje case as soon as possible.

c) Finally, there is a third judgement when it is stated that the private revelation "*consists in the non-supernatural*". The difference between this judgement and the one just mentioned ("*does not consist of the supernatural*") lies in the fact that in this third case the judgement is definitive. From the examination carried out, it is definitively confirmed that the phenomena of a manifestation which seemed supernatural in reality does not come from God; it could be a manifestation of preternatural, diabolic events or falsifications by people.

The case of Fatima

And so we enter into the context of Fatima. That of Fatima is a private revelation which, according to the judgement of the Church, "*consists of the supernatural*".

The Church has expressed this judgement through the most careful verification undertaken by the Bishop of Leiria, who examined the events in the 1930s, at the time of Sister Lucia. He interrogated the little shepherd children, especially Sister Lucia, who he also asked to write down everything she remembered. The *Memoirs of Sister Lucia* stem from this request by the Bishop; out of humility, she would never have written them on her own initiative. In this regard Sister Lucia remembered one thing: at the time of the apparitions she could neither read nor write, but Our Lady asked her to learn to read. At the time she did not understand the need, but when the Bishop made his request, then she understood why Our Lady wanted her to learn to read and so to write. Thanks to her strong memory, Lucia, despite being illiterate, remembered everything and put everything down in writing.

From the Bishop of Leiria, the case passed to the Apostolic See, with Popes Pius XII, John Paul II and Benedict XVI. These Popes made the Message their own and presented it as addressed by God to the whole Church. Therefore the Message of Fatima became worldwide, and has spread to the whole Church.

We recall that, among the Popes, the first to respond to the requests of Our Lady at Fatima about the consecration of Russia to Her Immaculate Heart was Pius XII in 1942. He gave to the Church the Holy Mass in honour of the Immaculate Heart of Mary and fixed its celebration for 22 August. The response of a Pope to a message is the clearest, most decisive authentication that this message comes from God; in our case, that Our Lady has spoken at Fatima.

After Pius XII, all the Popes of the 20th century have shown themselves to be favourable towards Fatima. Paul VI was the first to go there in 1967. Then John Paul II, true apostle of Fatima. Arriving in this blessed place, he repeated the consecration of the world and Russia to the Immaculate Heart of Mary, at least twice, united with the bishops. In 2010 it was the turn of Benedict XVI who, in his homily, referred to the mystery of Fatima as a still open prophecy for the whole of the Church.

So it is clearer than ever, then, that there is the very first guarantee of the Church's Magisterium of the Holy Father about this supernatural event. He responding with the consecration itself assured that it was really Our Lady who asked for it. So the Fatima apparitions are supernatural manifestations.

Now, what must be done by someone who wants to respond to these requests from Our Lady? They must welcome this Message seriously, make it their own and live it with faith; to the extent that that is done, Fatima will be a sure help for salvation. This, ultimately, is the guarantee of the Church.

So as well as the authentication by the Church's Magisterium, at Fatima we have another very important proof, to which we will return, and it is the life of the little shepherd children, above all of Saints Jacinta and Francisco. A holy, heroic life, of two little children, something astonishing! A child of 7 years of age who offers her life as a holocaust for the salvation of sinners, seeking all ways possible to offer sacrifices, to respond to Our Lady's requests: isn't this an heroic fact? And then another child, 9 year-old Francisco, so full of zeal for Jesus and for souls. Two children, both illiterate, moved by a supernatural inspiration responded to these requests accepting in everything the will of God, which consisted in their so premature deaths, with a resolute desire to sanctify themselves and to sanctify souls, for which they offered themselves. The lives of the little shepherds is therefore another proof of this truth of Fatima, of the sign that at Fatima Our Lady really did speak.

A further definitive guarantee, on which the Church's judgement was also based, is the miracle which happened at Fatima, for which Lucia asked Our Lady. Our Lady said: *"In October...I will perform a miracle for all to see and believe"*. And so it happened: on 13 October there was first of all torrential rain, everyone was soaked by the water. Suddenly, the sun dried all the bystanders and began to spin. As well as the miracle of the sun, again there was the apparition in the sky of Our Lady and then the Holy Family; then again Our Lady of Carmel with the Scapular in her hand.

This is a premise for understanding Fatima and above all to be convinced that following Fatima does not deceive us. On the other hand, it would be harmful and misleading to reject it. This is very important for our Faith. The same is true for following Lourdes and La Salette: they are both private revelations, but stamped with the Church's approval.

Whoever goes to Fatima, with the guarantee of the approval of the Church, knows with absolute certainty that Our Lady has spoken there, that what Our Lady has said comes from Heaven. It is therefore an additional proof of our Faith. Fatima confirms the Gospel. What we believe by Faith, the Most Holy Virgin let the little shepherd children see, and they were so taken by this Message that they lived the few subsequent years in such an heroic way as to be finally proclaimed Saints. At Fatima, therefore, it is right to speak of "wonders".

WHY THE FATIMA-EVENT?

Now we come to the Fatima-event from an historical point: why did Our Lady appear at Fatima?

The Message of Fatima is very rich, it has many aspects, but they are all linked with the period of that time and open wide a new horizon on subsequent times and the time still to come. We will now seek to have a global vision of them, keeping for ourselves at a later time a specific in-depth examination of the various aspects.

The Lady dressed in White came to Fatima in the distant year of 1917. What was happening in that year?

War as punishment because God punishes

We have seen how the Fatima apparitions were prepared for by the apparitions of the Angel, who describes himself as the Angel of Peace, the Angel of Portugal, and appears three times preparing for the apparitions of Our Lady. The Angel taught the little shepherd children the reparation prayers. Then on 13 May 1917 Our Lady appeared.

That year 1917 was a very important historic year. The First World War was underway. In the third apparition Our Lady said:

> *"If what I say to you is done, many souls will be saved and there will be peace. The war is going to end; but if people do not cease offending God, a worse one will break out during the pontificate of Pius XI. When you see a night illumined by an unknown light, know that this is the great sign given you by God that he is about to punish the world for its crimes, by means of war, famine, and persecutions of the Church and of the Holy Father".*

In fact, the Second World War followed. In the *Memoirs of Sister Lucia* it is written that the little shepherd children, even though they were so small, understood that war was allowed by God as punishment for the sins of humanity.

Today people are scandalised at the thought that God can punish by war. But no one raises the real problem which goes back to the early stages. What starts a war? Hatred, very often economic interests and new geopolitical aspects. But hatred, interest, are motivated by selfishness, by perverted conscience, by adoration of material things, even when someone says they are religious. At the origin of all this is a mystery of iniquity, a terrible mystery, which is called "sin". Responsible for sin is the sinful person, the selfish person, who thinks only of themselves, of their own interests, the person who does not want communion but division. This is the terrible reality of sin! The sinful person, due to this perverse will, provokes war and destruction.

So it is asked: where is God in all of this? Can He not stop war? Could He not extend His hand and intervene to confuse the arrogant? Rather we should ask ourselves: why does the human person continue to sin? Why, despite having received life from God, the grace of being a child of God, freedom, does the person continue to offend God? Why continue to insult God, to trample on His Commandments and turn against the holy things of God? From that stems permission for war, precisely to punish these injustices.

That year of 1917 was the year of the World War, but in Russia in October there was the Bolshevik Revolution, which gave rise to a way of understanding the things of humanity completely outside every perspective of God, of goodness, of freedom and all things most sacred. Starting from the false concept of material poverty – war to provide bread for everyone is envy for the wealth of a few – every social and civil order was subverted. There was a starting presupposition: the true oppression of humanity is God, the One who really makes the difference! To free the human person, it is necessary to free the person from God, killing God. Condemning God to be forgotten, offence against Him also became irrelevant. And even in the Church, which in some of its representatives and important moments would not hide being charmed by that inhuman ideology. That is why Our Lady of Fatima asked for the consecration of Russia: She was giving advance notice that that ideology, which would then spread throughout the whole of Europe and the Americas, would in effect subvert the very way of thinking and living, would threaten human existence itself, condemning it to worship material things. It would lead to placing ideologised poverty first and above the laws of God and proper Faith.

In fact Russia as a nation has greatly changed nowadays. Sometimes, however, one has the impression that its alienating and Marxist characteristic has remained not just in the conscience of the Left-wing parties, but has even penetrated deeply into the Christian conscience of many in the Church, pastors and faithful.

Fatima, too, "confounds the proud"

By appearing at Fatima the Immaculate places before us the sad reality of the sin of men and women which unfortunately continues to threaten human existence. Sin is the real reason for every tragedy. A sin which persists, a sin which spreads, which becomes almost the norm of life due to this ideological revolution. The only barrier to evil is the redemptive sacrifice. However, unfortunately there would be no one or almost no one to offer themselves to God in reparation and as redemptive oblation for the many. Also because with the theology of liberation – the theological variation of the Marxist revolution – and with its premises it would no longer be necessary to adopt a theology of reparation and oblation, but it would be necessary to "fight" at a social level to transform men and women not through grace but through war.

Our Lady, foreseeing all of that, comes to ask three little children: "*Are you willing to offer yourselves to God...as an act of reparation for the sins by which He is offended?*" The logic of Fatima is the same logic as the Gospel: God confounds the arrogant, humiliates the powerful and raises up the simple, the small, the humble: through those little ones He confounds the pride of the arrogant and those of a certain theology. At Fatima, against a power so immense as was the power of the revolution, the ideological power of Europe without God, in the face of this huge empire, the Soviet Empire, Our Lady countered with a weapon almost ridiculous to the eyes of the powerful: three children, three innocents, asking them to want to do God's will, to want to offer themselves to Him to save souls. In the eyes of the world this is truly ridiculous: three children against such a powerful monster! Sadly even some theologians mocked Fatima. To them it seemed absurd that the consecration to Our Lady could cause the fall of Communism, of such an extensive octopus. And so many mocked this message as something infantile. A simple consecration, a simple offering of self, would cause the destruction of this wicked power. Was it possible? But the Gospel is this: God who confounds the pride of the arrogant, of the powerful, through the simplicity, through the humility of the little ones, of a little one, Jesus.

What does Our Lady ask these three children? She does not ask them perhaps to do great things, but to do what no one wants to do. She asks them to make themselves victims, to become an offering like Jesus in reparation for the sins of humanity which continue to be the reason for world destruction, for war, for calamities, for ideology, for the persecution of the Church, for hunger, for poverty. She simply asked for their agreement: "*Are you willing to offer yourselves to God...as an act of reparation for the sins by which He is offended?*".

Thus one can also understand the apparitions of the Angel, aimed at preparing this most fundamental concept of reparation, of self-offering in reparation for sins. While the Angel taught the prayer of reparation, Our Lady made the request of the offering in reparation, which the little shepherd children embraced generously, making a continual offering of themselves.

From all this one can understand that what is really indispensable, and that Our Lady asks us seriously, is the prevention of sin along with its reparation.

At Fatima we can understand that sin is not something abstruse or insignificant. Sin, as disobedience and rejection of God, rejection of His Commandments, has tremendous repercussions in the history of humanity and in our lives. Sin is the cause of humanity's ruin, and, even, if it persists, is the cause of men and women's eternal ruin, which is Hell, and which Mary Most Holy in the July apparition let the three children see as a sea of fire into which were plunged *"demons and souls in human form, like transparent burning embers, all blackened or burnished bronze, floating about in the conflagration"*.

Someone has said that it is just an imaginary vision, even, on the part of Lucia. In her fantasy as a child, she constructed this image of a lake of fire which burns, and where there are demons and the damned. But it is not a fantasy, it is not an image constructed by the simplicity of a child.

These children, in their innocence, did not even know what the word "Russia" meant, for example. When Our Lady spoke to them about "Russia", they thought, not knowing about geography, it was a lady called Russia. Herein lies the beauty and genuineness of the Message. Clearly, not knowing Russia, they would not even have been able to "imagine" such a tremendous reality as Hell. And then why would the children have imagined Hell and not imagine instead a never-ending place of toys and games? Obviously, it is not an imaginary construction, but a real vision. At Fatima one learns what today no-one wants to remember, and that is that every sin, every offence against God's Commandments is the cause of humanity's greatest misery and, if this sin persists, is the cause of men and women's eternal perdition.

The cornerstones of Fatima

While Our Lady revealed to the three children this tremendous mystery – on the one hand people's sin and therefore the punishment which God inflicts so that they might be converted (war) and on the other hand what He inflicts when people do not convert (Hell) – at the same time She is the bearer of the hope of salvation. What salvation? That sweet salvation enclosed within Her Immaculate Heart, synthesis of the whole of Revelation.

In the face of the sad reality of Hell, such a terrifying scene, Our Lady offers this alternative. In fact, it is God Himself who offers it. So Our Lady says to Lucia: "*God wants to establish in the world devotion to my Immaculate Heart*". This is very beautiful: it is not an initiative of Our Lady, since every revelation is always God's initiative. As we have said, the judgement according to which the Fatima-event "*consists of the supernatural*" reveals that at Fatima there is the very initiative of God: it is God who sends His Mother, it is God who at Fatima wants to establish devotion to the Immaculate Heart of Mary as a way of salvation. Mary's Heart is the antidote to perdition: it is anti-hell.

So on the one hand there is disaster, death, war, sin, Hell; on the other, refuge, salvation, redemption, what God gives as the solution to evil: the Immaculate Heart of Mary, consecration to this Heart.

Our Lady subsequently asked Sister Lucia – as the Angel had already forecast in the July Apparition – on the "Five First Saturdays of the month" to put into practice this Fatima act of reparation. The "Five First Saturdays" were asked for the reparation of sins which pierced the Immaculate's Heart like thorns.

Summing up, we can say that Fatima has two absolutely fundamental aspects or "cornerstones":

a) *reparation* and therefore taking sin seriously as an offence against God and the destruction of humanity;

b) the *Immaculate Heart of Mary* as refuge, as space of salvation, as the place which God wants to save people from eternal ruin.

In the end, these two aspects could be united precisely in the Christian vision of the consecration to Our Lady making Her mediator of salvation for our brothers and sisters. The giving of oneself to Our Lady makes one aware of the need, the urgency, to free brothers and sisters from sin, to save them from eternal perdition.

Fatima teaches this: to be united with the Mother of Heaven, with Jesus, in the offering of self for one's own salvation, for the salvation of our families, for the salvation of all sinners.

We cannot live our Christian life in a carefree manner, with the pretence that, deep down, "God has saved us", He does everything. Instead, Fatima repeats that to be Christian means to feel in oneself this need of redemption, of liberation from the terrible snare of sin, to collaborate with Christ and the Virgin Mary in the salvation of all. Fatima reminds all the admirers of Luther, old and new, that there is no salvation without a sincere conversion and collaboration with God. Of this collaboration the Virgin Mary is the prototype and pinnacle.

An anchor of salvation

But it could be asked: in His majesty does God really need the Immaculate Heart of Mary? One of the objections raised against Fatima is exactly this: the consecration to the Immaculate, is such a simple instrument of piety able to achieve God's will for the whole of humanity? Once again God responds by humiliating the arrogant and, this time, humiliating the ecclesial arrogance of some who wanted to put devotion to Our Lady to one side as something outmoded, to make room for a "more intense" devotion, for a "more mature", "more adult" Faith, which would renounce these forms of piety, of "devotionalism", such as devotion to Our Lady, or even consecration to Her.

For some parish priests and bishops it would be scandalous even to speak about consecration to Our Lady; they say that we are already consecrated to God through Baptism and therefore it would be idolatry to consecrate ourselves to the Virgin Mary, too. We must not forget that at Fatima God Himself spoke through the Immaculate Heart of Mary. It is God who sends His Mother and it is really Him who humiliates the proud and gives us the Immaculate Heart of Mary.

Someone has said that prior to 1917 devotion to the Immaculate Heart was somewhat unknown and so how can it be integrated into the Church's Tradition? It is a somewhat unfounded objection because devotion to the Heart of Mary was already part of the Church's spirituality. There are many saints, especially in the period 1600-1700, who describe its devotion. Suffice to think of the greats of the French School.

In summary, we can say that consecration to the Immaculate Heart of Mary – which means *consecration* to the Immaculate, to the person of Mary, implying *devotion*, that is the offering of self – is a given fact of the Faith of the Church from ancient times. Right from the Church Fathers this consecration to the Immaculate has been lived. Suffice to recall that the oldest Marian prayer, dating back to the 3rd century, found in an Egyptian papyrus, is the *Sub tuum præsidium*: "*We fly to your patronage, O holy Mother of God*". To find refuge under the protection of Mary means putting oneself under Her mantle, that is, to give oneself to Her, to consecrate oneself.

At Fatima, Our Lady spoke in an explicit manner of this "finding refuge" in Her Immaculate Heart. In the second apparition, that of 13 June, she said to Lucia: "*My Immaculate Heart will be your refuge and the way that will lead you to God*".

From all these elements we notice how God's action at Fatima is in harmony with His own action in the Gospels and throughout the whole of Sacred Scripture. It is the same God who is acting and who out of love for His children gives to Fatima the most precious thing He has, the anchor of salvation which is the Immaculate Heart of Mary.

Anyone who goes to Fatima must ask Our Lady for this special grace to understand what a great gift it is being consecrated to Her Immaculate Heart as way of salvation; to understand the grace of being all Hers, of totally belonging to Her, of being able to enter into this salvific space of God which means escaping ruin, destruction, war, sin, Hell, perdition.

The Immaculate Heart of Mary is that pure space of God, it is that uncontaminated garden where there is no shade of sin, where God reigns, because Our Lady has never been slave to the devil, not even for an instant. That is why God gives us the Immaculate Heart of Mary, because it is the sole totally immaculate refuge where He lives and in which He wants to save us.

A gift from the Cross

At Fatima God explained once again the great gift of His Mother at the foot of the Cross. The problem is that so many call into question precisely the fact that God gave us His Mother at the moment of His crucifixion. It is understood by many as a fact of material necessity: since Our Lady no longer had a Son, it was necessary for someone to take Her into their home, to look after Her, and so John took Her with him to give Her hospitality. This is the vision of the Protestants, shared, however, by many Catholics, who, to reduce the necessary presence of Mary in our lives, say that it is a word of Jesus circumscribed by that event, by that immediate need. Instead, at the foot of the Cross there is a revelation of God who gives Mary as our Mother: *"Woman, here is your son'. Then he said to the disciple, 'Here is your mother'"* (*Jn* 19:26-27).

At Fatima, the Son of God offers us once again that heart as "refuge", it is we who must enter Mary, as at the foot of the Cross, exactly as John did: *"And from that hour the disciple took her into his own home"* (*Jn* 19:27). This does not really mean he took her into his house. It is translated that way in English, but in the original *"to take into oneself"* assumes the meaning "to take among the things most dear, to take Mary into his own life". So it is a spiritual welcome, which is the same as saying that one is acceptable to God when one enters into Mary, when Our Lady takes us amongst Her dearest things, like children, like Her property. And then we become children of the Immaculate Heart of Mary.

Fatima confirms this great gift which God has bestowed by giving us His Mother. The Immaculate Heart of Mary is a synthesis of the whole of the mystery of Mary Most Holy.

We will return to this to understand the most profound significance of the terms "*Heart*" and "*Immaculate*" (from which comes the adjective "*immaculate*"). We will discover that "heart" expresses the most intimate thing, the centre of the Marian mystery which is offered by God as salvation, as refuge, and "*immaculate*" points to the purity, to the new uncontaminated creation.

A sure refuge

Our Lady said to Lucia: "*My Immaculate Heart will be your refuge*". In a century as terrible as the 20th, God Himself has given men and women the refuge proportionate to the evils and the disasters of that time. At a time of such a great crisis in Faith and of great historical revolution, of ideologies which have threatened and provoked war and destruction, God has offered the Immaculate Heart of Mary as refuge. It is important to note that this refuge, the Heart of Mary and above all consecration to it, is a gift of God's Providence in this historical moment.

To respond to some very old objections, this "*Heart-refuge*" is not an absolute novelty of Fatima. God's insistence on giving us the Immaculate Heart at this moment means that while the whole Church, from the outset, has been consecrated – in certain centuries more than in others – to this Heart, now, in a clear manner, thanks to a supernatural even though private revelation, God has expressly declared that our salvation passes through consecration to the Immaculate Heart of Mary. So thanks to Fatima, God makes His will clear. And so it can really be said that everything that comes before is used as preparation for the Fatima-event.

The whole of life and also the Faith of the Christians of the first centuries was already directed towards the mystery of Mary and indirectly to Her Heart as Mother. Devotion to Mary experienced favourable progress and important dogmatic development. Thanks also due to a terrible revolution, God has spoken explicitly in our days, offering an excellent remedy for the evils and the necessary medicine to heal them: Our Lady, Her Immaculate Heart. Fatima indicates progress in the theology of the Immaculate Heart of Mary alongside Her clear revelation as a salvific instrument. Thus we learn that the Immaculate Heart of Mary is the sole way to God.

In humanity's total confusion in a world where God is hated, there is a desire in consciences to kill God and Religion – which will also quickly be followed by the depreciation of life and things most sacred – men and women can be saved by a maternal hand, can only be taken again by Our Lady's hand to be brought back to God. Once the sense of God has been destroyed in the consciences of men and women, it would be impossible to return directly to Him, men and women would not be capable of doing so. So the Lord, in His goodness, offers this remedy, this refuge. The Immaculate Heart of Mary comes from Heaven: it is the Mother who puts out Her hand to us to lead us back to God. Therefore it could well be said that, in a direct and supernatural way, Fatima reveals the way to God, the path of always, but which is now revealed as being the only way: either this path is travelled, or all hope is lost; either refuge is taken in this Heart, or existence itself continues to be threatened.

We recognise the grace of this gift of Fatima. God Himself has consecrated this way making us understand that this is the path on which we must set out if we want to go to Heaven. So devotion to Our Lady can no longer be optional, it is not an option depending on personal devotion, on one's own inclination towards devotion to Jesus or Mary Most Holy. Devotion to Mary is not even a cultural inclination, as some theologians have said: Latins would be more inclined to it while Anglo-Saxons would happily do without. It is essential to understand that the Immaculate Heart of Mary is the sole way to God. Whoever does not take this path finds themselves in serious difficulties in reaching God. Fatima teaches that the Immaculate Heart of Mary is the final remedy against destruction, Hell, perdition. Either Mary – the paradigm of human collaboration with God – or emptiness forever.

FATIMA AND THE LOGIC OF THE MYSTICAL BODY OF CHRIST

It is fundamental to examine in depth what Our Lady said in order to translate it into concrete works of conversion and sanctification. In this section we will explore the Message of Fatima to understand a key aspect of the mystery, which is Our Lady's continual request – and before Her, the Angel's – to the little shepherd children to offer themselves in reparation for the sins committed by humanity.

A number of times Our Lady spoke to the little shepherd children about offerings and sacrifices:

> *"Are you willing to offer yourselves to God to bear all the sufferings He wills to send you, as an act of reparation for the sins by which He is offended, and of supplication for the conversion of sinners?"*

The Message of Fatima repeatedly emphasises this aspcct: the solidarity of all men and women in Christ and therefore the need to make reparation for the sins committed against God and against the Immaculate Heart of Mary.

This is contrary to our mentality, our way of thinking. Today especially there is widespread individualism, where each person thinks of themselves, lives for themselves. And the most serious thing is that people think that a sinner sins for themselves, that the person responsible for the evil is solely the person who committed it. Instead, at the heart of Our Lady's request is the concept of Church, mystical Body of Christ, the concept of communion in Christ, as Saint Paul stated: *"We do not live to ourselves, and we do not die to ourselves. If we live, we live to the Lord, and if we die, we die to the Lord; so then, whether we live or die, we are the Lord's"* (*Rom* 14:7-8). Just as we are one in Christ in goodness, unfortunately, we are together in evil, too. In other words, evil, like the good committed by someone, reflects on others, too. Therefore an individual's actions – be they good or evil, and so sinful – reflect to the good or to the detriment of the whole Body of Christ which is the Church, and, even more generally, on the world, on the whole of humanity. In effect, from envy, from sin, from hatred of one, two, three...war stems. From a good action of a small child who offers himself to God stems the salvation of one, of two, of so many. This is the logic of the communion in Christ in the one Body which is the Church.

With the Message of Fatima we must understand the need, the importance of the offering in reparation, of being united with others, because one is united with others, forming with them one body. That is why Our Lady asked the three children to offer themselves to remedy the sins committed and for the salvation of sinners.

The Most Holy Virgin did not show the children Hell simply to frighten them, but to let them know that *"many souls go to hell, because there are none to sacrifice themselves and to pray for them"*. Hence She asked them, innocent children, to offer themselves to God in reparation for these sins and for the conversion of sinners. To this invitation the little shepherd children immediately replied: *"Yes, we are willing"*. And so, by offering themselves and by their sacrifices, they have implored from God the salvation of others.

Whoever offers themselves to God implores the salvation of sinners

Deep down, this is the mission proper to Fatima and, if we like, the mission of the Christian: to be one who makes reparation.

With Fatima one cannot think just of oneself, with the excuse of having many sins for which to atone. Yes, clearly there is a need to atone for one's own sins, but to be one with Jesus and with Our Lady necessarily includes becoming someone who makes reparation for the sins of humanity.

It could be argued: but is it possible for my sacrifice to redeem the sin of another whom perhaps I don't even know? Yes. What is the origin, what is the model of this supreme reparation? Christ and Mary. Jesus offered Himself as sacrifice to God for the salvation of all. And why has God accepted this sacrifice for the redemption of the whole of humanity? Because it was the only sacrifice pleasing to God, the sacrifice of the Son of God, who offered Himself to God for the redemption of humanity. It was the only sacrifice worthy of God, to which His Mother, Mary Most Holy, united Herself inseparably, becoming our Co-redeemer. At the moment of His agonising Passion, She was united to Jesus in an inseparable way. Thus, Jesus and Mary offer to God this most sweet sacrifice, a sacrifice of Redemption, that is, of liberation from sin. From the sacrifice of Jesus and Mary has emerged the salvation of the whole of humanity.

Is there a need to offer one's own sacrifices, too, if Jesus has already done all He could? What is the point of our sacrifices if there has already been the most perfect sacrifice of Jesus, Son of God? Meditating on the Message of Fatima one learns once again about the need to be active in redemption with Christ. Of course, Christ has done everything; there is nothing we can add, because we are not perfect mediators like Christ, who is the unique perfect Mediator between God and humanity as God made man, who has reconciled us with God by offering Himself. Therefore, if Jesus has done everything, we must complete in our flesh what is lacking in the sufferings of Christ – as Saint Paul says – on behalf of his body, which is the Church (cf. *Col* 1:24). It is the mission of Christians, who must complete with their lives, their offering, not what is objectively lacking, meaning that which Jesus did not do, which would be absurd, but what is lacking at a subjective level; to *complete* in the sense of *implement*, to ensure that the most perfect Redemption of Jesus reaches their own lives and those of their brothers and sisters to be saved. Thus we build up the Body of Christ, His Church; we ensure that it *grows* in numbers and above all in grace, becoming saviour of many others.

Jesus has accomplished Redemption in an objective manner, that is, has put into practice all that was necessary to redeem us. But this does not mean that salvation is automatic, that men and women are automatically saved since Jesus has put salvation into practice. It is necessary to obey Christ and freely allow ourselves to be saved by Him, therefore collaborate in this Redemption, otherwise there is no salvation. Men and women must state their *yes* to Christ and persevere with grace in that *yes*: this is co-operation. That is stated very clearly by Saint Augustine: "*God, who created you without you, will not save you without you*" (*Sermo* CLXIX, 13). Eternal salvation is eternal communion with God, free from sin; for this communion, our conscious adherence to God is necessary. My freedom is certainly able because it is first *healed* and then *raised* by grace. By grace I am free from sin and therefore I can free myself, with the help of divine grace, from all the obstacles which separate me from God.

Objective Redemption is an immense treasure, it is like a room full of treasure which, however, is closed (otherwise thieves would be ready to ransack it). To enter this room containing God's treasure which Jesus has won for us, that is, salvation, it is essential that I enter by getting the key. Grace gives me the necessary energy to set out, but the key does not fall from the skies: I have to look for it, I must get hold of it. This key is Our Lady. Whoever finds the Virgin Mary finds salvation. Therefore it is essential to find the key to get into this room. So objective Redemption will be implemented, because I take part in it, I make it my own, after having opened my heart.

Hence the need to be collaborators with Christ, because not only we but many men and women – we are bound in Faith to our brothers and sisters, being one Body in Christ and thus we become collaborators in the salvation of our brothers and sisters – find this path, find Our Lady to enter into God's treasure.

For this reason at Fatima Our Lady asked the three innocent little shepherd children to offer themselves in sacrifice. By their offering, they became "little Jesuses", they did what Jesus did with Mary, in their own small way. Jesus did it universally, once and for all. They did it in a small, but truly extraordinary way, at that historic moment, for all the souls which God's grace wanted to save through that offering.

How do you offer yourself to God?

The offering of the little shepherd children must be our offering. That is how we must imitate them. We, too, must become an offering to God for the salvation of our brothers and sisters. If there is a soul who offers him or herself to God, who gives themselves for the salvation of their brothers and sisters, so many other ignorant souls, who are against God, can be saved. How many? How many experience God's Mercy: certainly a lot.

However, many people also say 'no' to God, rejecting His Mercy. For this reason Our Lady showed Hell with the souls plummeting into it. They fall into Hell so easily because they are constantly living in sin, they no longer have the strength to get up, they do not want the help of grace, because they do not have people who pray and offer themselves for them so as to soothe their hearts.

The Message of Fatima guards against this risk which is very current in our society, because, if men and women simply become more cruel, selfish, self-sufficient, the way to perdition is always easier, smoother, it becomes an inevitable consequence for a great portion of humanity. What is the remedy? The offering of self in Christ to become in Him *another Christ* for today and for tomorrow.

We have understood that we must offer ourselves to God. Now we must unite another aspect to this offering. What does it mean to offer oneself to God? How did the little shepherd children understand the meaning of this offering? What did they have to do? The little shepherd children understood it in a very beautiful and simple way: they had to transform everything in their lives into a sacrifice, into an *offering* to Jesus. For example, that of not drinking when they were thirsty. One day – it is told in the *Memoirs of Sister Lucia* – Jacinta was really exhausted. The whole day under the sun, she could no longer even stay on her feet. The little shepherd children were exhausted from the heat and wanted to drink. Lucia went to a nearby village to ask for a little water. When she returned, she invited first Francisco and then Jacinta to drink. After a day under the burning sun, both, however, refused to drink. *"I want to suffer for the conversion of sinners"*, was Francisco's response; *"I want to offer this sacrifice for sinners, too"*, Jacinta replied in turn. Immediately Lucia understood and poured the water into a hollow in the rock, renouncing that little bit of water and letting only the sheep drink it. The first sacrifice they conceived was to give their snacks to the sheep: *"Let's give our lunch to the sheep, and make the sacrifice of doing without it"*. And they satisfied themselves with the acorns from the oak trees because they were much more bitter than others, thus offering a sacrifice to Our Lady for the conversion of sinners. Usually the offering was simply accompanied by a prayer: *"O my Jesus, this is for love of You, for the conversion of sinners...."*. We, too, must learn this prayer when we offer a sacrifice to the Lord.

They strived in many other ways to offer a sacrifice. Jacinta was gifted. For example, when she was seriously ill in hospital, she could not stand even someone talking beside her, because she had really piercing headaches, but with humility, with patience she offered even that continually having to listen to so many people who went to visit her, who wanted to speak with her and see her. She did not have the physical strength, because she was very ill, and the only prayer she succeeded in saying was: "*O my Jesus, this is for love of You, for the conversion of sinners....*".

That is what it means to offer a sacrifice: to deprive oneself of something and offer that privation and suffering to God and thus make reparation for sins, which are offences caused to God by someone who, instead, does not want to miss anything and ends up being their own boss. There are many opportunities for offering sacrifices, it would be enough to offer all the acts of patience that have to be exercised during the day; all the acts of strength often required so as not to respond badly or not to speak in vain; to renounce being critical, prejudicial, or wasting time in front of the television, or useless programmes, trash-television; to renounce wanting to know everything, to be informed about everything and to gossip. To reject spending hours and hours connected to the internet, ending up living a virtual life, which is not to live at all. Sacrifice is to love silence and so reject the dictatorship of noise and claptrap which pollutes our soul.

"Sacrifice" is not an ugly or even theologically incorrect word. It is an almost frightening term, because it seems that it refers to something negative, which limits us, deprives us. That is not the case. "Sacrifice" – from the Latin "*sacrum facere*" – means "to do something sacred", "to render an action sacred", that is, to *consecrate* that action to God. Of course, this *consecration* implies a *transformation* of my being, a denial of my vices and my passions to raise me to God. That consists in the fact that to carry out a sacrifice is always to *make holy* something by separating it from worldliness, from profanity and thus purifying it to raise it to the sphere of the divine. In such a sense sacrifice is tied to "suffering" or to "penitence", but its aim is the intimate *change* of something, of an action and, in the end, ourselves. Without sacrifice there is no sanctification, or, as the Letter to the Hebrews states, *"without the shedding of blood there is no forgiveness of sins"* (*Heb* 9:22). Jesus did it first in order to give us an example.

All actions can be made holy if they are offered to God. Even the simplest of actions which includes a rejection, a denial, can turn into an offering to God and become sacrifice, that is, it is made holy, it is done for God, it is consecrated and offered to Him. So our actions – but also the actions of others, which often we must endure and it is necessary to do so patiently without resisting so as not to make the sacrifice useless – if offered to God acquire an infinite value, become salvific, redemptive actions, which benefit so many in need of prayers. This sacrifice manifests one's own love for Christ, because love lies in this: in the renunciation of something for the one loved. Sacrifice, which is prayer raised to God, becomes request for salvation. It is incense rising to God and imploring goodness for others.

That becomes possible because in Jesus there is only one Body, one thing. That is why it is important to understand the logic of the mystical Body which is the logic of the communion of all the members in one body. According to this logic, to commit a sin, even deep down, in secret, involves a break, a stain which reflects to the detriment of the mystical Body of Christ. The sin of one person damages the whole Body and the good of one, the good action done by one is to the benefit of the whole body of Christ.

It is essential to understand this teaching for us, too, to respond to this call to conversion and reparation. Subsequently we will see how conversion and reparation must always be united to the Immaculate Heart of Mary: everything must pass through Her Immaculate Heart. In fact, Our Lady, in calling for reparation, at the same time offers the key to enter the treasure room, Her Immaculate Heart.

THE FIRST APPARITION: 13 MAY 1917

After these lengthy introductions, we now enter into the reality itself of Our Lady's apparitions to grasp the salient points of the messages which the Holy Virgin passed onto the little shepherd children.

The apparitions began on 13 May 1917 and continued for six consecutive months, until October, according to the desire expressed by the Lady dressed in White to the little shepherd children.

There was a thunderstorm, and the claps of thunder were frightening the little shepherd children who led the sheep a little further to find refuge; suddenly, above a holm-oak they saw a Lady dressed all in white. It was Lucia who asked her: "*Where are you from?*". "*I am from heaven*", the Lady replied. On hearing such a reply, the children will certainly have asked themselves how come a creature from Heaven had come to visit earth. The figure in white answered:

> "*I have come to ask you to come here for six months in succession, on the 13th day, at this same hour. Later on, I will tell you who I am and what I want. Afterwards, I will return here yet a seventh time*".

In fact she would reveal herself personally again to Lucia to ask for the "Five First Saturdays of the month" in reparation for sins. The children, who studied the catechism with their parents, immediately understood that "Heaven" was a metaphor aimed at describing Paradise, the Kingdom of God. So Lucia, intrigued, asked: "*Shall I go to heaven, too?*". "*Yes, you will*". Then again: "*And Jacinta?*". "*She will go also*". "*And Francisco?*" This time Our Lady's response was different: "*He will go there, too, but he must say many Rosaries*". It was Jacinta who reported these words to Francisco, since he was the only one of the three who was unable to hear Our Lady's words. Right from the first apparition, Mary Most Holy, in a similar way to the Angel, asked:

"*Are you willing to offer yourselves to God and bear all the sufferings he wills to send you, as an act of reparation for the conversion of sinners?*"

Overall, this is Our Lady's first request. Even before revealing Her name and the reason for Her visit, She makes this request, wherein lies the heart of the Message of Fatima and which will be repeated in other apparitions, too. It is a request of love but pressing, urgent! Almost like saying: it is necessary that you offer yourselves to God. But Our Lady does not impose it, but asks: "Are you willing to offer yourselves...?". She asks these children for co-redemptive help, that is, a "free collaboration" in the redemption of men and women. Our Lady asks for this help right from the outset to collaborate with Her and the response of the children was very simple: "*Yes, we are willing!*"

If instead Our Lady had asked us, perhaps we might have immediately put up resistance with numerous questions: "But what does it mean? What do I have to do?". We are so brave in always saying "no", finding so many excuses so as never to get involved!

These three little children were innocent, spontaneous, simple, but not foolish or superficial, in fact they were most profound children; gradually they learned to understand, but they really understood what "to offer oneself" meant and applied it in such an astonishing and generous fashion, conceiving of so many sacrifices to offer themselves to God.

Someone might reply by saying that Our Lady had chosen three children because simple children always say "yes" and probably they were not even aware of what they were doing. Obviously, that is not the case. It is important to underline that at Our Lady's request Lucia enthusiastically replied on behalf of all three: "*Yes, we are willing*"; it is a thoughtful but generous yes. In the face of this beauty from Heaven one could not say no.

In this apparition the children did not yet know that it was Our Lady, but saw in front of them a most beautiful Lady dressed in white, who revealed to them that they would have much to suffer, but that God's grace would always help and comfort them. Having said this, Our Lady opened Her hands, which up to that point had been joined. That is why the little shepherd children always prayed with their hands joined. That is very important. Even through the apparitions of the Angel the little shepherd children learned that prayer raised to God must always be done with hands joined, exactly as Our Lady did when She presented Herself to them.

In our prayer, too, the hands are important. "Joined hands" means that my prayer rises into God's presence, goes up to Heaven and I am in God's presence, conscious that my prayer must rise to the divine throne. There is never any need to have your hands hanging down when you're at Mass, when you receive Holy Communion: it would be a sign of distraction, of ignorance of what you're doing, of spiritual slovenliness. Our Lady teaches the children, through Her manner, how to pray. And from then on they always prayed on their knees with their hands joined.

Opening Her hands, She poured onto the children a beam of light which streamed from Her hands. So powerful was that light streaming from the hands of the Virgin Most Holy that it made "*us see ourselves in God, Who was that light*", said Lucia. The children realised from the outset that it was a supernatural presence. Immediately, due to an irresistible impulse, they knelt and repeated the prayer of adoration to the Most Holy Trinity taught them by the Angel: "*O most Holy Trinity, I adore You! My God, my God, I love You in the most Blessed Sacrament!*"

Finally, Our Lady recommended that the children recite the Holy Rosary every day with devotion, to obtain peace for the world. Having said this, She slowly left them, beginning to go up towards the East, until She disappeared in the light of the sun. This is only the first apparition, but already there is a clear overview of what will be the continuation of the apparitions and the awareness itself the children will have of this Lady and her requests.

Right from this first apparition the little shepherd children intended not to reveal anything of what had happened; that would have doubtless caused confusion in their families, aroused people's curiosity and the children would have found themselves in serious difficulties. All three spoke about this, but little Jacinta, so innocent, was already repeating along the way: "*Oh, what a beautiful Lady!*" Lucia reproached her, stating that in doing this she risked not keeping the promise. And that's just what happened; she first revealed things to her parents, and this caused great apprehension on their part and subsequently serious difficulties, major problems. After all, God was also using this simplicity to begin to shake people up, ensuring that this Message was gradually made known, understood and received by others.

THE SECOND AND THIRD APPARITIONS: 13 JUNE AND 13 JULY 1917

It was in the second apparition, on 13 June 1917, that Our Lady revealed a secret about the little shepherd children: Jacinta and Francisco would soon go to Heaven, while Lucia was still to remain on earth because, as Our Lady said, God wanted to use her to make the world aware of a special secret: the Immaculate Heart of Mary.

The central apparition was then in July, when Our Lady revealed to the little shepherd children the three parts of the Secret: the first part concerned the vision of Hell; the second, the request for the consecration of Russia to the Immaculate Heart of Mary: the remedy which God gave to the terrible evils of war and atheist ideology; the third part we got to know in 2000 and concerned the vision of a field where there lay so many lifeless bodies of martyrs and a ruined city on a hilltop.

This third part of the Secret is an overall reading of the history of the Church and of humanity, even if it is ever clearer that there is still a piece missing to complete the mosaic of the Secret, above all to pass carefully from the second part to the third, avoiding being left with a text which leaves Our Lady's other words hanging, inserting an unusual "etc.". A link is missing between the Faith which will be preserved in Portugal and the vision of the devastated city. Perhaps the city will be devastated precisely because there will be a lack of Faith? And will the Faith be preserved where a soul, a place, will become that merry Portugal which welcomed the hope of Fatima?

In any case, in the third part of the revealed Secret is contained the vision of an Angel about to strike the earth with a flaming sword, ready to bring justice for all the sins committed, which now cry out for justice in the sight of God. But a maternal hand holds back that sword: it is the Immaculate Heart of Mary which stops God's anger railing against humanity.

There follows the vision of an immense field, where can be seen so many dead religious, priests, bishops and also lay faithful: martyrs killed out of hatred for Christ. Then a hill on top of which there is a Cross; at the foot of this hill there is a person dressed in white who is about to climb it, setting out towards the Cross. This person dressed in white – Sister Lucia would reveal it to be the Pope – is struck and dies. The Angel with the flaming sword repeats three times: "*Penance, Penance, Penance!*".

From this vision can be learned on the one hand the heartfelt appeal to penance – the sole remedy against the spread of evil – and on the other the Church's situation down the centuries and internally: a Church decimated by so many deaths, so many persecutions and, we might add, taking up what the Holy Father Benedict XVI said, a Church shattered internally due to the sin of its children, of the sin within the Church. A sin which is even justified and so is no longer believed to be so. This is the sin which kills, the sin of those who have been called to be guides and pastors of the people of God. A Church which, through the false teaching of some or of many, contributes to self-destruction, causing the ruin of souls and of bodies. Who cannot think that this vision refers precisely to what is happening in the Church today? Bishops against Bishops, Cardinals against Cardinals, priests who from time to time re-write the Missal to say Mass according to the tastes of the time. An internal struggle on decisive questions of faith and morals: at stake is the very future of the Church.

This is a vision which alludes to the historical reality but, at the same time, makes us contemplate with hope the powerful intercession of Mary Most Holy on behalf of the Church, the great hope for all, the triumph of the Immaculate Heart of Mary: "*In the end, my Immaculate Heart will triumph*", said the Virgin after having shown this terrible vision. However, the certainty of the triumph should not allow us to sit back in an inactivity which would reveal a spiritual ignorance, thinking of being able to trust solely in the certain triumph, without any personal commitment. Our Lady stated that in the end Her Heart will triumph, but in the meantime the Church is an immense field of the dead. In the meantime, the enemy is at war with the Church and seeks to destroy it from within. It will not prevail, because "*the gates of Hades will not prevail against it*" (*Matt* 16:18), but the Church which receives blows is – as Cardinal Ratzinger said in the *Via Crucis* in 2005 – "a boat taking in water on every side", because it is taking blows and is no longer able to react: with sin harbouring within the Church it self-destructs; with so many doctrinal and disciplinary deviations the enemy gradually threatens its end from within and causes the destruction of souls. The souls ruined and lost forever due to scandal and heresy are no longer redeemable. They are lost forever. That is why it is necessary to react, to get involved: we must save souls from physical, moral and spiritual destruction. Definitive destruction is in fact eternal Hell.

Our Lady ensures that Her Immaculate Heart will triumph, but in the meantime if one does not become aware of this sad situation the Church will grow ever weaker and so many souls will be lost. Hence the responsibility of each person to ensure that the wolf does not remain loose in the enclosure to devour the sheep.

Our Lady, through the three visionaries, also enables us to see this reality. We cannot say that this is not the case or that the Message of Fatima has already concluded. For this reason Fatima is a Message which tests the Church today, the whole of the Church, each of us. We cannot pull back. The reality is this: the Church is reduced to a field devastated by the enemy. How many Christians have been persecuted throughout the whole world, how many Christians cannot freely profess their Faith and have been killed in the name of religious intolerance! So many other Christians, instead, are prey to a somewhat do-good attitude, of relativist thought which intoxicates the West. No one is bothered anymore about God, eternal salvation, the Sacraments, but people live like animals, intent solely on material things. In fact, animals are preferred to human beings. This is a life which is equivalent to spiritual death, a death always and forever.

If this is the sad but true reality of the Church – what is there of the Church desired by God as the Ark of salvation for humanity? – then it means that the Message of Fatima is a most topical message, which tests us. What is our response? Will we still say that Fatima is a pious private revelation for the usual devotees? We must respond as did the little shepherd children: making our own this desire to offer ourselves to Our Lady for the salvation of so many brothers and sisters.

Therefore, to ensure that humanity sets out on the way to salvation, the way of the triumph of the Immaculate Heart of Mary, it is necessary to make ourselves collaborators with the Immaculate for the salvation of our brothers and sisters.

Guarantee of protection? Yes, but not for long

Our Lady wants to protect us from this wave of fire – as Padre Pio would also say: *"Beware the avalanche of fire!"* – from the flaming sword which is being wielded against humanity. Our Lady is there as a good Mother, but She, too, is subject to the will of God, therefore She will stay this hand as long as it is possible, but if evil continues to spread She will no longer be able to stop the avalanche of fire, the hand of God. Justice will be required for sins. So we should not delude ourselves that the Holy Virgin will be a guarantee of salvation for us, so that we continue to do what we want, even! The fact that Our Lady is there to stop this hand should alert us: we see what awaits us if we do not convert. This sword could fall sooner or later against the world. And in fact Sister Lucia, as reported in the visionary's last book, based on the archive material from Coimbra monastery (*A Pathway Under the Gaze of Mary*, World Apostolate of Fatima), would see the sword of God hurled against the earth touching its axis so as to make the whole world jolt. Oceans, seas, mountains: everything was turned upside down and buried. A truly apocalyptic vision. Here are the words of Sister Lucia (chapter XIII, about the writing of the Secret):

> *"I felt my spirit flooded by a light-filled mystery which is God and in Him I saw and heard: the point of the flame-like lance which detaches, touches the axis of the earth and it [the earth] shakes: mountains, cities, towns and villages with their inhabitants are buried. The sea, rivers and clouds leave their bounds, they overflow, flood and drag with them into a whirlpool, houses and people in a number unable to be counted; it is the purification of the world from the sin in which it is immersed. Hatred, ambition, cause destructive wars"*.

Then, however, Lucia hears a gentle voice which says:

"Down the centuries, one faith, one baptism, one holy, Catholic, apostolic Church. In eternity, Heaven!" The word Heaven *fills my soul with peace and happiness".*

This word "Heaven" also fills our hearts and gives us courage. But reflecting on what has already happened, is it not perhaps true that this lance is already being cast on the world? How many earthquakes! How much turmoil! Turbid tsunami of every kind. To read these events in the light of God's Providence, which is justice and mercy, means to believe, once again, that God punishes. That sin itself is humanity's punishment. But today it seems one cannot say that God punishes, but rather "admonishes". However, admonishing is already within the perspective of punishment: a father first admonishes and then punishes the child for his or her good. What people do not want to recognise is that God can punish and also use natural disasters – which He does not wish directly, because He only desires our good, our salvation, but He allows them – to admonish and punish us and to make us understand that, if we will not convert, we will all perish in the same way (cf. *Lk* 13:3). Is it not already a tremendous punishment to live in a carefree manner, convincing ourselves that God does not punish us? What else must we see to understand it? Let us take this warning seriously. Let us offer ourselves day after day in reparation for the sins which draw this lance ever closer to humanity and which cause turmoil and death.

The wealth of messages

In the May apparition we saw that Our Lady's first request was: "*Are you willing to offer yourselves in sacrifice for the salvation of sinners?*", and the children, in their simplicity, said "Yes".

The little shepherd children began to encounter so many difficulties, above all at the heart of their own families, dismayed due to the influx of so many pilgrims. The parents feared that their children were deceived or the matter was simply a suggestion or even a devilish reality; so they sought in every way possible to convince them they were self-deceiving, and wanted to avoid at all costs the scandal of so many people coming from all corners and then for the deceit to be revealed.

In June the parish priest of Fatima interrogated the children, but they were unable to reveal the Secret Our Lady had entrusted to them. The parish priest's first reaction was incredulity: it could not be a supernatural reality coming from Heaven. Only time would reveal the truth of these apparitions.

In August the children were even imprisoned by the mayor of the town, who sought in every way possible to dissuade them from believing what he held to be self-suggestions and he wanted the children to declare publically they had been deceived. Despite so many ploys, aimed at getting the children to confess to the supposed deceit, the children in their simplicity did not lie, they knew well they had really seen Our Lady.

But let us return to the July 1917 apparition which is one of the richest for the supernatural content of the Most Holy Virgin's teachings.

After arriving at the Cova da Iria, the Lady dressed in White showed Herself again. While usually it was Lucia who spoke to Our Lady, this time, ecstatic at the vision, she was unable to speak; it was Jacinta who aroused her: "*Come on, say something, Our Lady wants to speak*".

The Virgin Most Holy repeated Her request that the Holy Rosary be recited daily to obtain peace in the world. She then asked them to go there every month and said that in October She would perform a great miracle, so that everyone might believe.

Our Lady's request about the recitation of the Holy Rosary emerges frequently. During the apparitions, usually Lucia asked Our Lady for the grace of healing of the sick; at the request for the healing of a lame person, the Virgin replied that She would not heal them, but they had to recite the Holy Rosary faithfully with their family every day. Other people, too, on whose behalf Lucia asked for grace, had to say the Rosary. In this apparition as well Our Lady returned to the request of self-offering in reparation for the salvation of sinners:

> *"Sacrifice yourselves for sinners, and say many times, especially whenever you make some sacrifice: O Jesus, it is for love of You, for the conversion of sinners, and in reparation for the sins committed against the Immaculate Heart of Mary".*

Our Lady asked that every sacrifice offered to Her be accompanied by this prayer.

At a certain point during the apparition there was a small cry: *"Oh!"*. That cry from Lucia – as was explained subsequently in the revelation of the Secret – was a cry of fear: in fact, having asked for self-sacrifice for sinners and having taught them the prayer in the offering of a sacrifice, Our Lady showed the little shepherd children Hell.

The three parts of the Secret of Fatima which make up this vision were only revealed by Lucia after 25 years, at the request of the competent authority, the diocesan Bishop of Leiria, who, on 31 August 1941, asked her to put the first two parts of the Secret in writing in her *Memoirs*.

The competent church authority believed – after 25 years – that the time had come to make known the first two parts of the one Secret, comprising three parts. The third part, which we got to know (partially?) in 2000, was instead put in writing by Lucia at the end of 1943, after great suffering, experiencing a sort of incapacity to transcribe that terrible vision. This third part was given to the diocesan Bishop and finally reached Rome in 1957 at the request of the Holy Office. A question which arises reflecting on the lengthy silence about the third part of the Secret is this: if its content is, all things considered, what we now know, why was it kept secret for more than half a century and why did two Popes – John XXIII and Paul VI – believe it inappropriate to reveal it, and instead kept it locked in a drawer? What is there particularly "scandalous" in what has been revealed? The assassination of a Pope and the reference to 20th century martyrs?

The vision of Hell, certainly not a fantasy

As we have already indicated, the first part of the Secret concerns the vision of Hell. We will try to understand this tremendous reality, which is a truth of Faith and which Our Lady highlights here so that the real danger which is hanging over humanity and over men and women might be understood, that if men and women do not convert and welcome Her requests they will perish in this eternal fire into which, sadly, many souls are already falling. It is faced with this sad vision that Lucia gave that cry of fear.

Our Lady opened Her hands, as She had done in the previous two months, and from them came a ray of light which seemed to penetrate the earth and the children saw as it were a sea of fire, into which were plunged demons and souls in human form, like transparent burning embers. These were dragged into the air by the flames which issued from the souls themselves and along with great clouds of smoke they fell back on every side, amid shrieks and groans of pain and despair which made the children tremble and horrified them. The demons could be distinguished by their terrifying and repellent likeness to frightening and unknown animals, black and transparent like burning coals.

> "*This vision*", said Lucia, "*lasted a moment. And thanks to our good Mother from Heaven, who had anticipated in advance with the promise of bringing us to Heaven (in the first apparition), otherwise I believe we would have died out of fear and terror*".

74

In the May apparition, in fact, Our Lady assured the little shepherd children that they would all go to Heaven; in June, on the other hand, She stated that Jacinta and Francisco would go there, while Lucia would only join them later.

It is good to reflect more profoundly on the reality of Hell which Jesus speaks about repeatedly in the Gospels (this reference occurs at least 18 times) and which at Fatima, through God's providential mercy, was revealed in a sensitive way to the children. Such a tremendous truth is about the definitive condition of those men and women who die in a state of mortal sin, without repenting, without asking forgiveness from God. The Church in its Magisterium has always taught and teaches that the souls of those who die in a state of mortal sin, that is, of serious offence against God, immediately descend into Hell to be punished with different punishments.

Some have said that this is about a fantastic imagination on the part of the children of Fatima, because, they say, Hell could not materialise in their sight. And deny completely that there are flames in Hell, that there is a certain place, a sea of fire where the damned have been immersed. Instead, it must be said that it is not simple imagination, but a real and proper vision of a certain materialisation of a tremendous eschatological reality about which the Gospel speaks. If the vision of Hell is imaginary why shouldn't that of Our Lady be so, too? Hell consists of two most painful punishments:

a) estrangement from God (the pain of loss);

b) the pain of eternal fire, which never goes out (the pain of feeling).

The sad reality of Hell lies in the definitive estrangement from God in the state of eternal separation from Him and it is also marked by the pain of eternal fire, which Jesus speaks about in the Gospel: "*You that are accursed, depart from me into the eternal fire*" (*Matt* 25:41), as testified by the apparition.

To enable us to understand that Hell is not the reminiscences of an ancient doctrine, already present in the mythology of the Greeks and of all ancient peoples, that is the "Hades" as kingdom of the dead where all souls went, Jesus, in his divine teaching, does not simply make reference to a Hades, but to "*Gehenna*" (for example, *Matt* 10:28). Gehenna was a place in Israel, at the time of Jesus, where the rubbish of Jerusalem was burnt and where therefore there was an ever-burning fire. In such a way the truth of Hell was separated from every cultural residue and expressed well the new teaching of the divine Master. In fact, Hell was inaugurated with the Lord's Redemption and precisely with his descent to Hell, when the just were liberated while the wicked were condemned for ever.

Hell and Mercy

Many people react to the possibility of eternal damnation by placing blind trust in God's mercy. When all is said and done, isn't Hell contrary to God's mercy? Could God definitively condemn a soul to Hell? It seems – in today's Church – that the condemnation of a soul to Hell excludes or limits God's mercy, His forgiveness.

To respond to these questions it is essential once again to reflect on the tremendous reality of sin which is not something innocuous or banal. If sin, and therefore the sinner who commits sin, is condemned by God in the name of His merciful justice, that demonstrates that sin is so terrible that when it becomes persistence, when it becomes rejection of God it can only be punished by estrangement from God. The vision of Hell reminds us that we have a responsibility, that of our actions, since moral actions, the daily choices, are not irrelevant, but determine our lives in relation to God and to our neighbour. When we choose, in every action, we choose good or evil; either we choose God or perdition. We choose to remain with God when we do good and we observe His Commandments, or we distance ourselves for ever from Him when we choose what is contrary to His will, sin. Therefore, we cannot live irresponsibly, like permanently immature children.

Just as good renders us eternal and capable of being with God, so that we become in some way like Him by obeying Him, so evil renders us like demons, proud, arrogant, ambitious, selfish, self-sufficient, to the point of saying "*I will not help*". This obstinacy in evil can only be punished by definitive estrangement from God, in Gehenna, in the eternal fire.

Nowadays, someone, navigating in the seas of relativism, might think: so God *imposes* Hell on men and women, given that so many people do not believe in Him. In the spreading apostasy in which we live there should be a sort of general condemnation. In truth, Hell, like Paradise, is a free choice. God does not violate freedom, but gives us the grace to go along with freedom as with goodness. Being sinners, being wounded and inclined to evil, we are more inclined to evil than to good. God, in His great goodness, provides every help so that our rebellious and wounded will can freely choose Him and therefore choose salvation. But when men and women reject God's help, when they reject God Himself, they simply choose what is not God; if this choice remains resolute and fixed, at the moment of death there can only be Hell.

We know how much this sad reality is no longer taught today for fear that souls may be frightened. It is feared that not only children may be frightened, but especially grown-ups, and the risk is that they may never set foot again in church. In homilies, too, every reference to Hell has disappeared, since it is thought that God in His mercy has closed it or that if it is there, because Jesus speaks about it, we don't know if there is anyone there.

This is another subtle objection enjoined by many: Hell would be empty. It is certain that only the devil goes to Hell, but if we say that there is someone in Hell we would be evil, we would be condemning rather than forgiving. This is false! You can't hope for the damned. You can't hope against the clear words of the Gospel! When hope is not based on faith it ends up separating mercy from truth and justice. That is, mercy is condemned to becoming a word which comforts but is bereft of meaning.

Jesus speaks about Hell and also says that there are *many* who unfortunately set out on the path of perdition, since *"for the gate is wide and the road is easy that leads to destruction, ... the road is hard that leads to life"* (*Matt* 7:13-14). Many people choose the way which is most comfortable, but this comfortable path leads to perdition. For this reason Our Lady came to Fatima, because many set out on the comfortable path and do not realise that instead the path to Heaven is very narrow. There is a need for conversion, to renounce sin to go to Heaven.

To stubbornly believe the idea of a "retirement Hell", many bring into discussion *tout court* the truthfulness of Fatima or seek to provide a more symbolical explanation of Hell, which certainly does not correspond to Hell as condition and metaphysical place, that is, as real possibility of men and women's perdition, a doctrine now believed to be superseded by love (of the good God of the New Testament).

To put forward the theory of uninhabited or empty Hell is like excluding the reality of Hell itself and contradicting the dogma of Faith. So we must think that when Jesus speaks to us about this reality and this state of perdition He does so only to exhort us to be good. But if Hell were just an exhortation, then why shouldn't the exhortation to love, to be joyful, also be, too? It is wrong to say that Hell is empty. When Jesus, in the universal Judgement, will say to the just: *"Come, you that are blessed by my Father"* (*Matt* 25:34) and to the wicked: *"You that are accursed, depart from me into the eternal fire*" (*Matt* 25:41), He is referring to real people. We do not know exactly who, but we know that some will go to one place and some to another. Jesus' words are not simply metaphorical, but real, just as the Incarnate Word is real.

To teach that the door to salvation is narrow, to be gained with effort, offering oneself in sacrifice to God, Jesus tells us that His Blood, His Redemption, has been offered for "*many*" (*Matt* 26:28; *Mk* 14:24). Jesus' words over the chalice of wine, which becomes His Blood, are about the "*many*" to be saved; that Bread, His Body, is offered for "*many*", not for all; not because Jesus wants to exclude someone because there is a predestination of some for salvation and others for perdition, but because that Blood offered for all will not be efficacious for all, because not everyone wants to drink of it, not everyone will accept it, but many will deny it, many will reject it. "*For many*" means that many will drink that Blood and will be saved, but many others will unfortunately damn themselves. The battle between good and evil will only end with the definitive separation of evil and good at the moment of the final Judgement.

A remedy for perdition

Fatima confirms what the Gospel says: "for the gate is wide and the road is easy that leads to destruction" (Matt 7:13).

Our Lady Herself, showing Hell to the little shepherd children, said to them:

> "*You have seen hell where the souls of poor sinners go. To save them, God wishes to establish in the world devotion to my Immaculate Heart. If what I say to you is done, many souls will be saved and there will be peace*".

There then is the sad reality of Hell and immediately the remedy: devotion to the Immaculate Heart of Mary. "If they will do what I say...". The Virgin will call for the "Five First Saturdays of the Month" in reparation for the sins committed against Her Heart and for the consecration of Russia and the Nations to Her Immaculate Heart. If all that were to be done, Our Lady guarantees salvation. Precisely, it was 10 December 1925 when Our Lady, appearing to Sister Lucia at Pontevedra, in Spain, formally requested the practice of the "Five First Saturdays of the Month". Sister Lucia writes:

> "Our Lady, as if to encourage me, rested her hand on the right shoulder, and as she did so, she showed me at the same time Her Immaculate Heart which she held in the other hand, encircled by thorns, and the Child Jesus said: Have compassion on the Heart of your most holy Mother, covered with thorns, with which ungrateful men pierce it at every moment, and there is no one to make an act of reparation to remove them".

Then Our Lady said:

> "Look, my daughter, at my Heart, surrounded with thorns with which ungrateful men pierce me at every moment by their blasphemies and ingratitude. You at least try to console me and say that I promise to assist at the hour of death, with the graces necessary for salvation, all those who, on the first Saturday of five consecutive months, shall confess, receive Holy Communion, recite five decades of the Rosary, and keep me company for fifteen minutes while meditating on the fifteen mysteries of the Rosary, with the intention of making reparation to me. In exchange I promise to assist them at the hour of death with all the graces necessary for the salvation of their souls".

Our Lady assures Lucia that whoever undertakes this devotion is promised eternal salvation. These souls will be favoured by

God and like flowers they will be placed by the Virgin before His throne. One could ask precisely why Five Saturdays. Lucia in fact asked Jesus, who responded to her:

"It is making reparation for the five offences at the Immaculate Heart of Mary: 1) blasphemies against the Immaculate Conception. 2) against her virginity. 3) against her divine maternity and the refusal to recognise her as the Mother of all men. 4) the work of those who publically instil indifference, scorn and even hatred towards the Immaculate Mother in the hearts of children. 5) direct insults against Her sacred images".

The Message continues:

"The war [the First World War] is about to end; but they will not stop offending God, during the Pontificate of Pius XI a worse one will begin. When you see a night illuminated by an unknown light, you know that the great sign which God wishes to give to you is to punish the world for its crimes, by means of war, hunger and the persecutions of the Church and the Holy Father. To stop it, I come to ask you for the consecration of Russia to my Immaculate Heart...".

So another war is foretold as punishment of the world for its sins. War, and therefore famine, a persecution against the Church and against the Pope. To stop all that Our Lady asks for the consecration of Russia to Her Immaculate Heart.

Russia! We come once again to this theme which is so central to the Fatima event. This giant of ideological terror has spread its inhuman ideology, Communism, which falsely presented itself as an instrument of the social liberation of humanity, throughout the world. Hiding behind the beautiful words was a deep-rooted hatred of God, Religion, the Church, in the conviction that the true oppression of humanity is not the rich versus the poor, but Religion, the Gospel, the reality of an eschatological Hell presented by the Church. Men and women must free themselves from this religious vision of life to be finally free in this world. To be free from Hell beyond this life meant wanting to transform the "Hell down here" into an earthly paradise. The result was that a Hell in this life was created, too.

The founder of Communism, Karl Marx, presented himself as a new Jesus, wanted to be the true messiah, a social messiah, bearer of true liberation: liberation from Jesus Christ, from sin, from Hell, from perdition, things which, in his opinion, alienated men and women and distracted them from their true objective. In fact all these Christian terms were not rejected, but were overturned in their intra-world connotation: the only real sin became the exploitation of the poor, the so-called social sin. There was no need of God, nor Faith, but just the capacity to transform material into richness, even at the cost of shedding so much blood.

That is why Our Lady said: "I shall come to ask for the consecration of Russia to my Immaculate Heart"; She wanted to stop the moral destruction of society, caused by the increasing development of materialism which like an octopus gradually spread everywhere, starting from the Soviet Empire. Our Lady's request is a barrier to this empire of evil, to this empire of Lucifer, who does not want God to be heard but only himself, with the promise of false happiness. It is the same snare of original sin: to convince men and women that if they will listen to the diabolical directives they will become like God, they do as God and so will be able to choose themselves what is good and what is evil, without God deciding it, without God's Commandments. To oppose this destructive lie, Our Lady asked for the consecration to Her Immaculate Heart:

> "*If my requests are heeded, Russia will be saved and there will be peace; if not, she will spread her errors throughout*

the world, causing wars and persecutions of the Church. The good will be martyred, the Holy Father will have much to suffer, various nations will be annihilated".

But then, like a ray of light which disperses the clouds, Our Lady adds: "In the end, my Immaculate Heart will triumph" and concludes with these words: "The Holy Father will consecrate Russia to me, and she will be converted, and a period of peace will be granted to the world".

So, we can say that the only alternative to the materialistic de-Christianisation and tremendous atheistic secularisation remains the Immaculate Heart of Mary, the "refuge" and "salvation". "God wishes to establish in the world devotion to my Immaculate Heart". We understand how indispensable today is this divine alternative, at this time, to raise the world from extreme poverty and the Church from self-destruction.

We know that Russia has effectively spread its errors throughout the whole world. And we also know that this revolutionary process was followed by a process of increasing secularisation and dehumanisation, a nihilistic process which destroys everything which is truly human. Today we find ourselves in the face of transhumanism as a logical result of the subversion of all values in the name of a basic ideology: worship of material goods. We are witnessing the justification of death as a good for humanity, abortion and euthanasia as a need of the freedom of men and women, of the recognition of homosexual couples as respect of the rights of the person. In the name of a false liberty, everything which is contrary to men and women and therefore to God, to what God did in creating men and women, is justified.

This process of subversion leads to a flattening, a levelling of all the fundamental values of the life of humankind. There is a truly devilish pride which moves States, Parliaments to legislate in favour of private choices which have no relevance in the public sphere, while the good of all is no longer necessary, it seems that it is of no importance to anyone. In fact, the once so-called "non-negotiable" principles have practically disappeared from ecclesial vocabulary, because now everything is negotiable. And thus has not the path leading to perdition been made smooth?

Hence Our Lady's invitation, the remedy, the sole indispensable remedy, the anchor of salvation which She gives us to escape from this de-humanising danger, not to be swept away by the river of nothingness which drags everything towards the abyss. At this time of the Centenary of Fatima, we must consider carefully the prophecy of the Lady from Heaven. She offers us the alternative to destruction and to the abyss of the world and of the ecclesial whole. Towards the end of the July apparition Our Lady said, referring to what She had revealed: "Do not tell this to anybody". The little shepherd children kept the secret and, only at the express wish of the competent authority, Sister Lucia would put in writing the first two parts of the Secret. Then Our Lady asked again the little shepherd children: "Do you want to learn a prayer?" And She taught that prayer which we recite after every decade of the Holy Rosary.

> *"When you pray the Rosary, say after each mystery: O my Jesus, forgive us, save us from the fire of hell. Lead all souls to heaven, especially those who are most in need".*

It is again a request to the Lord of forgiveness and salvation from perdition. Thus ended the July apparition. The key point of this third apparition lies in this: on the one hand the vision of Hell, God's on-going justice; on the other hand, the remedy, the Immaculate Heart of Mary. So we must enter into the Immaculate Heart of Mary, take refuge in it with a life of faith, of hope, of charity, of adoration of God: "My God! I believe, adore, hope and love You". We enter into the Immaculate Heart of Mary, most pure place where God saves us and brings us to Paradise.

Consecration to Our Lady

We will focus now on the importance of the consecration to Our Lady, while we defer to the final section of the book the problem of the consecration of Russia. To be consecrated to Our Lady is an ineffable gift. It is possible to speak of two types of consecration: there is a simple consecration, made like an act of Marian devotion, and then there is a more specific and binding consecration, which in turn assumes various nuances, by reason of the proposed spirituality:

a) consecration to the Immaculate as Marian slavery according to Saint Louis-Marie Grignion de Montfort: the Christian is bound to Mary as a slave of love;

b) unlimited consecration to the Immaculate according to the spirituality of Saint Maximilian Kolbe: the Christian is called to become "instrument", "thing", "property" of Mary;

c) the Marian Vow of unlimited consecration to the Immaculate according to Fr Stefano M. Manelli: the vow gives to the Kolbian consecration, understood as becoming "instrument", even "nothing" in the hands of Mary, the character of *solemn promise*, although in the private form (made with one's own confessor or spiritual director) envisaged by the *Code of Canon Law*. Especially through this last level of consecration we are bound to a spirituality which is intimately connected to that of the Message of Fatima.

So what does consecration to Our Lady entail? Consecration in each of its forms entails love of Our Lady, the obligation to recite the Holy Rosary daily and to wear the Marian Medal or Scapular, to know Our Lady Most Holy, to make Her loved and to spread Her devotion. Above all, it is necessary to deepen awareness of Mary Most Holy, because you cannot love what you do not know. It is necessary to draw closer with greater intensity to Our Lady, to read a lot about Her, to collaborate in Her universal mission, which consists in spreading knowledge about Her and making Her loved in all accessible places, the home and the workplace, to make Her known and loved. The Message of Fatima, in a central way, consists in consecration to Our Lady. So it is good to respond to it through consecration. Without too much fear, deriving from a neo-puritanism which threatens our Catholic Faith.

It is true that Baptism consecrates us to God as His property; through Baptism we become "children of God", reborn through water and the Holy Spirit: we become the "temple of God". So we are of God. What of Our Lady? Is Marian consecration necessary? Our Lady's function, and therefore consecration to Her, is to be seen as a *way* to be able to go to God in the most perfect manner. We are consecrated to the Lord, but since Our Lady is the Mother of God, it is She who made Jesus and therefore the only one who can form Jesus in us. We consecrate ourselves to Her not to counter a creature to the Creator, but to find that creature who is so dear to the Creator as to shape Him as true man. The true Christian is made only by Mary. However, creatureliness is not enough.

We start from on High. Who is the Immaculate?

To understand the opportunity, the goodness, the need to consecrate oneself to Our Lady, it is necessary to remind ourselves of Her role compared to God. If we draw close to Our Lady just as to a simple creature, to a lady of the people, it is clear that consecration to Her would be nonsensical. In fact, if Our Lady were – as some might say – a "working lady", it would be even dangerous to offer oneself, to give oneself, to consecrate oneself to Her. Starting out

86

instead from a supernatural vision, we realise that Our Lady is, yes, a lady, a creature, but it is She who was predestined by God, from eternity, to be the Immaculate Conception to become, at the time set by God, in the fullness of time, the Mother of God. In God's salvific plan there is from eternity the Son, the Word of God, Jesus Christ, who was incarnated, desired by God for Himself regardless of the sin of humanity. In fact, when He wants, God wants things in a perfect way. He wanted the Son because the Son made man was the supreme perfection of creation which could summarise all of its perfection. From eternity the Father saw it, predestined it to be the Incarnate Word. And who is immediately close to the Incarnate Word? The Mother, through whom He was to be made flesh.

God sees from eternity the Son and, alongside Him, in union with Him, the Mother. The Son is God made man; the Mother is a creature, She, too, desired by reason of the Son. So the Lord bestowed a unique privilege: in His generosity – God is free to do what He wants with His gifts – He desired that the Mother of His Son, perfect lady alongside the Son, perfect man, be the Immaculate Conception, free from the stain of sin.

When we state the truth of the Immaculate Conception – a dogma of Faith defined by Pope Pius IX on 8 December 1854 – we believe that a creature, the Mother of Jesus and our Mother, from the first moment of Her conception was preserved from original sin, that is from that sin of disobedience to God committed by our Ancestors and into which we fall by the effect of our human generation, as descendants of one parent. Our Lady was a human creature and therefore had to be affected by this sin like all other men and women. Instead, by virtue of a privilege of grace, She was preserved from it. The Immaculate, therefore, is an exception, She is not a lady like all the others; a creature, yes, but unique.

Saint Maximilian stated that if you want to understand who Our Lady is, the Mother of God, you must understand who God is. You can never understand Our Lady thinking of Her like any lady. Similarly, you can understand consecration to Her thinking of Our Lady in this divine perspective, as "Immaculate Lady", as unique among women. When we pray to Our Lady with the words of the *Ave Maria*, we say "blessed art thou among women" (cf. *Lk* 1:42), because God has blessed Her in a most singular way, by reason of this "immaculateness". Our Lady can only be understood starting from God and not from humanity.

Nowadays, while dialoguing with the secularised world, there is the risk of diluting every supernatural reality. All that is divine and sacred risks being diminished by virtue of a deaf dialogue with worldliness, with society, with men and women of today. The dialogue seems a mere rhetorical exercise by those who already know from the outset that by now it is necessary to renounce every truthful pretence. Since men and women today find it difficult to think of things of God, even devotion and Faith sadly risk being impoverished. We self-condemn ourselves to looking. It seems we are looking, left bewildered.

On the contrary, at Fatima Our Lady asked to start from God. This Lady has come from Heaven. *"Where are you from?"* *"I am from heaven"*. These are Her very first words: if we want to know Our Lady, we must start from on high.

Eve and Our Lady: there is no comparison

We have said that Our Lady is the "Immaculate Conception", therefore preserved from sin. She never committed any actual sin, She was not able to, because She was without the original wound and therefore the original inclination caused by the sin of Adam and Eve.

It is often said: if Our Lady was unable to sin then She was not free. This objection, like so many others, reduces Our Lady to "anyone", because if She is also like us then we can be calm and bask in our sin. The problem is that for us freedom consists in doing evil. We measure freedom in relation to evil and not instead in relation to good. Freedom which commits evil is not freedom, but its abuse! We know full well and we realise it when we commit evil, when we sin. Only after having experienced the misery of sin do we understand that true freedom is not evil; true freedom is to do good, to love God with all one's heart and observe His precepts, the law of freedom. The Immaculate is totally free because She cannot offend God, but only love and respect Him.

Furthermore, speaking about the Immaculate Conception, it is interesting, to the higher exaltation of this Marian Privilege, to consider the difference between Her, Immaculate Conception, and Eve, the immaculate ancestor before original sin. They were both immaculate, but with a difference. By a simple comparison, Eve – Saint Maximilian would say – was "the white", Our Lady "the whiteness". Our Lady revealed Her name in Lourdes: "*I am the Immaculate Conception*", which was the equivalent of saying: "My very being is to be Immaculate". Eve was not the "Immaculate Conception", she participated in an immaculateness as gift of the original grace of God, but was a simple creature of the human race. Instead Our Lady is not like Eve. She was wanted by virtue of Christ, and so is much more than Eve. Eve was able to sin, because she had not yet been definitively confirmed in the grace of Christ. The Immaculate, on the other hand, by virtue of that by which Eve had also been created, had obtained all the grace of Christ, because She was to be partner with Christ in our salvation. Eve is a lady enriched by the grace of God, by a gift from which she then distanced herself, because she sinned freely; Our Lady was the same Immaculateness, that is the same *vessel* of all the redeeming grace of Christ, which was to re-establish the dignity of the children of God. This redemptive grace of Christ had been given to Her so that She might then distribute it to the children of Adam, those children redeemed by Christ, by the painful Passion of Jesus, to which She was united in a unique way, as Immaculate and Mediatrix.

89

There is no comparison between Eve and Our Lady! One can speak of similarity as regards being women: Our Lady, as Mother of God, is the "Lady", is the Immaculate who becomes the Mother of God, desired as Immaculate not just for Herself but also for us poor children of Adam, because as "new Eve", as ally and most faithful Spouse of the Redeemer, She collaborated in our salvation. We have been saved from sin by Jesus with Mary, by Jesus and Mary. This operation of Jesus and Mary together arises from an eternal predestination of Jesus and Mary, of the Redeemer and of the Co-redemptrix, that is She who was desired as Immaculate to be companion in Redemption, associate of Christ.

The presence of Our Lady in our lives is the presence of She who, Immaculate, is raised to the dignity of Mother of God and therefore has become our dearest Mother. When did She become our Mother? In a special way when She generated us in Her maternal pains at the foot of the Cross, collaborating in the supernatural re-generation of souls. While bringing Jesus, immaculate Lamb, to light, She did not suffer because She remained a virgin – it was an immaculate, virginal birth – but instead in bringing us to light on Calvary She suffered the pain of compassion. Jesus suffered in the body, Our Lady suffered in the soul. Suffice to recall the prophecy of old Simeon: when Our Lady brought Jesus to the Temple, he said to Her: "*and a sword will pierce your own soul too*" (*Lk* 2:35). This sword is the sword of grief in seeing the crucified Son, in participating in His Passion. Perhaps the greatest pain, the most piercing sword which goes through Her soul was above all our indifference, the persistence in our sins, despite the pain of the Son which was Her own pain. Just like the pain of a son is always painful for the mother, likewise for Our Lady: the pain of the Son was Her immense pain, Hers was united to that of the Son. If Mary Most Holy is the Immaculate, the Mother of God and our Mother, we belong to Her and She has maternal rights over us, having re-generated us as children of God to the supernatural life. We could not call ourselves Christian if Our Lady had not suffered with Jesus for us: we would not have obtained the grace of Baptism, nor that of conversion, nor any other Sacrament. Simply because we would not even have Jesus. Without Mary there is no Jesus!

The only path

Going over again the Message of Fatima we discover that grace to be good Christians, "old style" Christians we would say. It is a grace which arises from the Immaculate Heart of Mary. Our Lady has generated us as children. Now, every child needs a mother, so we, children of God, need a Mother. We have been engendered by the Passion of the Son, by the Compassion of Mary.

The monk Arnaud de Bonneval († 1156), friend and disciple of Saint Bernard, said there were two altars on Calvary: one was the body of Christ, the other the Heart of Mary. Two altars but one Sacrifice which rose up to God. The way in which Our Lady offered Jesus as Mother and Co-redemptrix is also the way in which Our Lady offers us to God. Consequently, giving oneself to Her becomes a debt of gratitude; it is awareness of what Our Lady has done for each soul.

Is there another more perfect path to God, another more worthy way, a way more certain than that of the Immaculate Heart? No! And this "no" can be inferred by reflecting on the history of Salvation, from which it can be concluded there is no more perfect way than that chosen by God Himself. Our Lady was wanted by God. She was not chosen by Christian piety, it was not popular devotion which down the centuries preferred to consecrate itself to the Virgin Mary, but God Himself who consecrated Himself to Her first, subsuming Himself in Her to come into our midst. In the same way, by consecration to the Immaculate, we go to God enclosing ourselves in Her. For this reason Our Lady says that She is the "sure refuge which leads us to God", because that is the holiest place where God alone lives, where there is only salvation, without any compromise with selfishness, with pride, with sin. God lives in Her, in Her Heart, in Her womb.

Therefore, consecration to Our Lady is a filial act of love which entails a boundless self-giving to Our Lady, consists in being fully aware of Baptism giving it a complementary Marian form, so that it may be experienced in a more integral manner, because She Herself renders us totally of God. Who is able to do this more than Her?

There are some very beautiful expressions in the Church Fathers who, in short, say this: in Her is realised an exchange between God and humanity. In effect, it is in Her womb that the *admirable trade* took place, the union of God with humanity. If we enter into the womb of the Immaculate, She will bring about this exchange once again: She who gave God to humanity, will give to us divinity, because She is the Mother of God.

A great Father of the Church, Saint Gregory of Nazianzus (c. 329-390), stated that whoever is separated from Our Lady is separated from the divinity, so they will have no access to God, will be unable to enter into His mystery. Here is a passage from *Letter 101* to Cledonius:

> "*If anyone does not believe that Holy Mary is the Mother of God [Theotókos], he is severed from the Godhead. If anyone should assert that He passed through the Virgin as through a channel, and was not at once divinely and humanly formed in her (divinely, because without the intervention of a man; humanly, because in accordance with the laws of gestation), he is in like manner godless*".

To separate oneself from the Mother of God with a heterodox faith is to separate oneself from God. The most beautiful way to be united with God, to love Him with all one's heart and in the most perfect way, living as good Christians, lies in giving oneself to Our Lady by consecrating oneself to Her. In the light of all that you can understand that the Fatima request is really a providential request for our time and is an offering of salvation. Consecration has its most remote roots in the Gospels, in Sacred Scripture and in the Church's Tradition, which has always known an act of giving to Our Lady. Fatima takes up again this most ancient tradition and develops it indicating its necessity and urgency. To consecrate oneself to Our Lady means taking refuge in this place of salvation belonging totally to God through Her. The grace of being consecrated to Our Lady is a grace which She bestows on Her beloved children. Anyone who wants to respond to the requests of the Holy Virgin must make themselves an apostle of the consecration to Our Lady, because there where one enters Our Lady one enters Jesus, therefore salvation. Whoever consecrates themselves to the Most Holy Virgin will no longer fall prey to the devil, the world and to the things of the world, to all that separates us from God. She is the shield which stops us from being separated from God, because She has never been separated, not even for a moment, from Him: She is always totally and only of God. Fatima teaches that returning to God is urgent. By taking refuge in the Immaculate Heart one goes certainly to God: to God alone.

THE FOURTH AND FIFTH APPARITIONS: 19 AUGUST AND 13 SEPTEMBER 1917

We have examined carefully the central apparition, that of July 1917, rich in theological and spiritual content. We have sought to deepen the mystery about which Our Lady speaks at Fatima, the terrible but true reality of Hell, and the alternative, which is the Immaculate Heart of Mary as refuge and way which leads us to God, the anchor of salvation which She Herself gives us.

The Lady dressed in White had asked the little shepherd children to go to Cova da Iria for six consecutive months, at the end of which She would perform a great miracle so that all may believe, and would also reveal Her name. It was customary at every apparition for Our Lady to ask the children to return, up to October.

In August – as we have indicated – something unique happened: the children were imprisoned, because the mayor wanted them at all costs to retract everything and state publically that they had been deceived. He decided to do so by force, frightening them and threatening to fry them in boiling oil.

The Fatima apparitions had shaken not just the town, but the whole of Portugal and pilgrims began to arrive from all over the country. If the little shepherd children had really lied, it would have caused such upheaval that the parents and the children themselves would have been threatened with death. That would have been a real scandal for the town.

It is important to emphasise another fact. The press and the political authorities were in the hands of Masons, who were tenacious enemies of the Church. Therefore a "fantasy" of this type would have given rise to Masonry attacking the Church in a profound manner, maintaining that the Church was based on a miraculous self-persuasion and Faith was nothing but popular superstition. Views which after all were already being spread but without specific proof.

Instead, thanks to the miracle of 13 October, it was precisely the Masonic press, in the newspaper *O Século*, which stated the truthfulness of the Fatima phenomenon, since even the Masonic journalists were eyewitnesses and so had to write in favour of a supernatural fact never before seen.

The children, despite the mayor's threats and the loss of their parents, were unanimous in testifying to the truth of the apparitions and above all in hiding the Secret of Our Lady. The mayor, like the parish priest, at all costs wanted the children to reveal it, but the little ones, who had received the request from Our Lady not to reveal it to anyone, remained firm in their intention.

While Jacinta, at the start, behaved like a real child singing here and there "*O, what a beautiful Lady!*" and let it be known that she had also received the order not to say anything, this time, in prison, did not give in to the pandering. The children were obviously persuaded by the truth of the vision. With the little shepherd children in prison, the Lady dressed in White was unable to appear at Cova da Iria on 13 August. She appeared, instead, on 19 August in the area called "Valinhos" (or Vila Nova), which means "little Valleys".

On 19 August everything was ready for the apparition and the children realised that the Most Holy Virgin was about to appear. The first question Lucia asked Her was: "*What do you want of me?*". Our Lady replied: "*I want you to continue going to the Cova da Iria on the 13th, and to continue praying the Rosary every day...*". At each apparition Our Lady asked them to come back on 13th and to recite the Holy Rosary daily, adding sometimes, as happened in September, to recite it with the special intention of asking God for an end to the War.

One Our Lady under different titles

Our Lady went on: "In the last month, I will perform a miracle so that all may believe". Then turning to Lucia, She said: "If they hadn't brought you to Vila Nova, the miracle would have been more sensational". Then She added that on 13 October "Our Lord will come, as well as Our Lady of Dolours and Our Lady of Carmel. St Joseph will appear with the Child Jesus to bless the world".

In the last apparition, in fact, the Holy Family were seen: Saint Joseph with the Child Jesus blessing; Our Lady of Carmel, presenting Her Scapular; and Our Lady in the semblance of Our Lady of Dolours. This is a characteristic fact of Fatima.

Why does Our Lady have so many different ways of revealing Herself? Isn't Our Lady one? It is interesting to note that at Fatima Our Lady also assumed different appearances, besides that of "Our Lady of the Rosary", a title proper to Our Lady of Fatima by which She will make Herself known. At Lourdes She said to Bernadette: "I am the Immaculate Conception", and She had the Rosary in Her hands; at Fatima She said "I am Our Lady of the Rosary". This is the correct connotation of Fatima, alongside Mary as Sorrowful Mother and Our Lady of Carmel. Why this variety of titles in just one vision?

Of course Our Lady is one. But appearing in different places and at different times, She assumes the appearances and titles in reference to a specific time and a specific place. What's more, the different titles highlight a diversity and wealth of doctrinal aspects linked to Our Lady: Our Lady Immaculate highlights Her mystery as Immaculate Conception and the absence in Her of original sin; Our Lady of the Rosary, the need to pray the Holy Rosary; Our Lady of Dolours, Her co-redemptive presence at the foot of the Cross; Our Lady of Carmel is Our Lady who gave the Scapular to Saint Simon Stock and presented Herself as the protector of Carmel, She who held in Her cloak Her Carmelite children and all devotees of Carmel, protecting them with Her maternal intercession.

This diversity does not multiply the oneness of Our Lady, but simply highlights the distinction in the various doctrinal aspects which refer to Her. There is certainly a Marian richness. This point is useful so as not to fall sometimes into a sort of ambiguity, asking ourselves: to which Our Lady must we pray? It is a question which hides an implicit rejection of Marian devotion. It is not a matter of praying to one of the Our Ladys. It is essential to pray to the one Our Lady, in the particular doctrinal richness which refers to Her.

We can pray to Her as Immaculate; we can pray to Her as Our Lady of Dolours or as Our Lady of Carmel. All these titles do not threaten the oneness of the mystery of Mary, but rather determine and distinguish it. The Laurentian Litanies, for example, are an anthology of praise to Mary venerated under different titles and in every time. Thus we see the truth of the prophecy of the Virgin: "All generations will call me blessed" (Lk 1:48), all languages, all peoples, all places. In the August apparition, the Most Holy Virgin guaranteed once again that in the last month She would perform the miracle. She then asked that with the money offered by the pilgrims two litters be made: one to be carried by Lucia and Jacinta with two other girls dressed in white; the other by Francisco and three other boys, covered by a white mantle. The rest of the money was to be for the feast of Our Lady of the Rosary.

A heartfelt appeal

In this month of August Our Lady insists on something very important. As usual Lucia asked Our Lady to perform miracles, healings. She replied that She would cure some of the sick during the year. Then with maternal care, veiled also with a degree of sadness, She once again exhorted the children to the practice of prayer and mortification. She added an important element to the Message:

> "*Pray, pray very much, and make sacrifices for sinners; for many souls go to hell, because there are none to sacrifice themselves and to pray for them*".

In their simplicity, the children asked for cures, while the Holy Virgin, veiled with sadness, asked for their prayers for a much more serious problem: many, many souls are lost, "*because there are none to sacrifice themselves and to pray for them*".

We have already spoken about prayer as offering, as solidarity on behalf of our brothers and sisters, on behalf of the mystical

Body. Once again Our Lady asked the children to *transform* every act, every attitude, every prayer, every offering in *reparation* for others. Let us say it again: the heart of the Message of Fatima is to *make reparation* for the sins of those men and women who, ignorant or naïve, sadly fall so easily into eternal perdition.

Sometimes it is asked: with so much ignorance of God and God's Law, couldn't men and women be excused rather than condemning them so easily to perdition? Our Lady at Fatima places before us a reality which today especially is obscured: *"Many souls go to hell, because there are none to sacrifice themselves and to pray for them"*. Ignorance is not such as to be excused always and at any cost. God has written in the hearts of every man and woman a moral law which *per se* does not justify ignorance. Of course I can be ignorant about this or that aspect (in a specific situation), but I must also do something to fill my gaps. To live deliberately in ignorance with regard to the good to be done, here and now, and the evil to be avoided is already guilty: it is a sign that in fact I am not at all ignorant but malicious. So to raise ignorance to a principle of guiltlessness is false and deleterious. God's Commandments are a most fundamental law of human action which has been inscribed by God in human nature, in the human person as such. Saint Paul, too, teaches this clearly: the pagans who are not living correctly, even if they do not know Jesus Christ, are accused by their own sins – just as the person who lives according to reason and does good is excused – because their reason is capable of seeing there is a natural good to be followed; instead, due to their perverse will they subvert the natural order and turn to sins which in effect contradict this natural moral law inscribed in hearts (cf. *Rom* 2:14-16). Ignorance here does not excuse condemnation.

So we must not be so superficial in stating that nowadays the absence of God is such as to be able almost to justify sin, precisely due to ignorance which people now have of God, from whom they are so distant as to no longer succeed in being aware of evil. Evil is almost an unconscious habit. In truth, ignorance which justifies can never be the desire to live comfortably without God. Ignorance justifies when men and women, while seeking truth, do not yet wholly know it, but in their hearts want to act with uprightness. It is a very different ignorance from that which cannot be bothered to know the truth – and therefore to conform one's life to God's Commandments – or even from that of someone who justifies not subjective ignorance of the norm, but depraved behaviour by virtue of the necessity of the situation. A step forward in "forgiving ignorance", towards the abyss.

Our Lady's phrase *"many souls go to hell"* makes us reflect. The fact that men and women today are increasingly without God does not justify the attitude of resignation and trust of those who think that in any case in the end God will be more merciful. The Lord has written the truth in the hearts of men and women. If it is more difficult, for those without grace, to conform to this truth, that does not exonerate from the need to be orientated towards God and to morally live good lives, doing good and avoiding evil with all one's strength. Distance from God certainly seduces in evil, gets used to it, but certainly is not to be self-absolved, even after a long process of discernment. Conscience is not a solitary entity which can decide from time to time what to do, what is good and what is not. Even the conscience of the God-less and the Faith-less is a human conscience, open to truth and love.

The mediating action

There is another factor which can be inferred from Our Lady's words. We have understood that there is this "obscuring" of God in the life of men and women, but it does not justify, and therefore does not exclude *ipso facto*, the perdition of the so-called ignorant or those believed to be such by virtue of mercy. Since, however, don't such people in the end have the strength, the courage, the clear awareness of having to return to God? When one is living in sin, everything contributes to remaining in sin. If there is no movement of grace aroused by prayers, aroused by the offering of self, these souls remain prisoners of evil, of their own *I* without God. That is why Our Lady says: "*Many souls go to hell, because there are none to sacrifice themselves and to pray for them*". Once again the insistence on the need to make offerings in reparation.

The offering of self on behalf of others is always a request of intercession with God, in Jesus and with Mary, because Jesus is the sole Mediator and Mary is the sole Mediatrix in Jesus. Our offering in reparation is an incessant request addressed to God for the good of our brothers and sisters who live in guilty ignorance of God, those who have not just rejected God consciously, but also those who do not do anything to shake themselves from the torpor of relativism; those who live without God because after all everyone does that, everyone lives like that. We must ask ourselves how much guilty ignorance of God is not rather the fruit of an *imitation* imposed by society, by fashion, by Facebook. To deny God is fashionable, it is easier, it is more comfortable: it is the only thought imposed on everyone, and it certainly does not justify and does not save. In fact, it gently falls headlong towards the abyss.

Therefore it is necessary to rely on the reparative offering which Our Lady requests. And this offering can only be a prayer raised to God, the sacrifice as self-renunciation to re-discover ourselves in a new way and so go out to meet our brothers and sisters in a new way. The renunciation, we were saying, is never finalised in itself, it is always a prayer which rises to God. This renunciation, united to the Hearts of Jesus and Mary, becomes, at God's side, a plea for the grace of salvation for so many souls who remain in guilty ignorance, an action of grace by which God can move and intimately touch the freedom of these people and therefore move them to conversion.

Our offering on behalf of souls becomes a mediation of graces, ensures that grace is introduced into this supernatural circuit so as to move the souls of prisoners of evil and enlighten them. And by this illumination finally so many souls are touched in their freedom, who up to now were uninterested in God, preferring a different, carefree life. This supernatural circulation of grace, by which God goes to touch intimately the freedom of men and women, is almost like a pin-prick which hurts, makes you reflect; it is an intimate small voice which says to the soul: "This is not good for you!" So finally grace, with our prayer and our offering, can prevail and encourage conversion.

Many times it is really mysterious to understand how a person, from a life of complete distance from God, moved by something which they themselves cannot even explain, realise they have to change their lives. They are moved to do so. This is supernatural grace which is acting: grace nourished by our offering, by our prayer.

It is precisely this that Our Lady asks the children of Fatima: to become mediators of salvation for people, to be mediators in Jesus and in Mary, mediators of the merits of Jesus and of Mary on behalf of people, by virtue of the sacrifices, by our prayer which becomes request and supplication of God. The prayer of the heart, as is said today, is not sufficient, meaning by this expression not so much the prayer taught us by the Desert Fathers, but a spontaneity which prays or perhaps an *I* which prays itself, incenses itself.

Unfortunately, in our secularised world there is a risk, and it is already at work, of reducing the whole of the practice of the Faith to the heart: suffice the heart is in it. So many justify their Faith, which is no longer nourished by prayer, nor by the Sacraments, pilgrimages, penance, sacrifice, with the slogan: "It is important that the heart is in it". Thus Faith is transformed into pure intimacy, into a Faith which is no longer seen, and so is dead, which does not work, because no external signs of it can be seen anymore.

It can seem strange, but the attitude, too, of joined hands is indicative of a Faith which is at work, a living Faith. It is also thus with the attitudes of prayer, like kneeling, standing or sitting in a composed not irreverent manner. It is not the same thing to stand or kneel in front of Jesus! These external attitudes contribute to ensuring that the prayer of the whole person can rise to God. If we accept the Message of Fatima, it will completely fill our lives of Faith so as to perfect the external attitudes, too, attitudes which have great significance at Fatima: lying prostrate, kneeling, hands joined, being in an attitude of request, of entreaty. Everything contributes to the true and holy attitude of prayer and intercession.

Examining the Message of Fatima in depth we re-discover precisely from Our Lady's words all those important qualities which our Faith must have. Our lives of faith and prayer must be nourished by intercession and intercession must be a complete offering of self, of soul and body.

What is necessary for Heaven

So we have reached the September apparition, a bit simpler, but nevertheless significant. In this fifth apparition, Our Lady places Herself as usual on the holm-oak and the first thing She asked the visionaries was to persevere in the recitation of the Holy Rosary in order to achieve the end of the war. She renewed the promise made on 19 August, and that is, that She would come in the last apparition with Saint Joseph and with the Child Jesus to bless and give peace to the world; then She asked them to come back on 13 October.

There follows an interesting fact which might seem almost ridiculous. The little shepherd children wanted to give some little objects to the Lady dressed in White: two letters and a small bottle of perfumed water which had been given to them by some brave pilgrims. Our Lady's response makes us think: *"These are not needed in Heaven!"* It is a response on which to meditate. Sometimes you want to give the Most Holy Virgin so many things, for example, flowers, necklaces, medals. Other times instead you want to take from Marian places something as a souvenir, preserving a flower, a bit of soil, a Rosary. All good things, which help our spiritual lives made of perceptible things. But let us remember: *"These are not needed in Heaven!"* It is essential to give to Our Lady what is most important: prayer, our love, charity, sacrifices, penance, our sincere conversion.

Lucia asked for other graces of healing. Here, too, as on other occasions, the Lady dressed in White said that some people would be cured during the year, others wouldn't. Why doesn't God heal everyone? So many times the Lord does not liberate us from the cross, because, as Saint Pio of Pietrelcina said: *"How many times would you have abandoned me, my son, if I had not crucified you"* (*Epistolario* I, p. 339). In effect it happens thus: when grace is immediately obtained, God is forgotten. *"Mortals cannot abide in their pomp; they are like the animals that perish"* (*Ps* 49:20). Men and women, when they have everything, forget God. On the other hand, the Lord, in His Providence, very often leaves us that suffering, that sickness for our spiritual good. Suffering is a gift to be able to participate closely in the redemptive suffering of the Lord and to remain nailed to Him, to His Cross. The Message of Fatima teaches us not to rebel against God and the Cross. Suffering is a pearl of love which Jesus gives to His friends.

Finally Our Lady reminds us that to go to Heaven what is really needed are not just objects, external things, not even physical healing or that grace which we need. What we need is – as the Letter to the Hebrews states – *"to approach with a true heart in full assurance of faith, with our hearts sprinkled clean from an evil conscience... . Let us hold fast to the confession of our hope without wavering, for he who has promised is faithful"* (*Heb* 10:22-23). Are we really convinced that the only things necessary on this earthly pilgrimage are faith, hope and charity?

THE FINAL APPARITION: 13 OCTOBER 1917

An apparition cannot be believed to be true unless there is a supernatural seal. The apparition is certainly from God if it is authenticated by a miracle. In October, Our Lady performed a great miracle.

At midday exactly they saw *"the flash of light and then Our Lady appeared on the holm-oak"*. It was pouring rain and the Cova was flooded. Despite the torrential rain, people continued to throng there, reaching about 70,000 people.

On seeing Our Lady, Lucia repeated her usual question: *"What do you want of me?"* In a subsequent account of the apparitions, towards the 80s, Lucia explained that for them as children it was good manners to address a stranger by first of all asking who they were and what they wanted. So these children, in all their simplicity, each time Our Lady appeared to them, put the same question.

During the apparitions, Our Lady had not revealed Herself, they did not know Her name and to describe Her they referred to Her by speaking of an "apparition" and a "Lady in White", or a "Lady dressed in White", just as the Virgin always showed Herself.

Finally in the month of October the apparition revealed Her name: *"I am the Lady of the Rosary"*, and She asked that a chapel be built in that place in Her honour. She had preannounced it: *"In October I will say who I am [and] what I want"*. In Lourdes, too, Our Lady revealed Her name: *"I am the Immaculate Conception"*, and asked Saint Bernadette for a chapel to be built in her honour.

A happy coincidence. Lourdes like Fatima is a prophecy, a supernatural gift which becomes source of grace for those who will visit such a place. Fatima was transformed into a great place of pilgrimage, because all the devotees who rush there can experience the grace of this place blessed by God. Hence Our Lady asked initially for a chapel where devotion to Her may continue to be cultivated. Then She recommended once again the daily recitation of the Holy Rosary, adding that the war was about to end and the soldiers would soon return to their homes.

"Do not offend the Lord our God anymore"

Lucia had received many requests from people to present to Our Lady, many questions, so she said: "*I have many things to ask you: the cure of some sick persons, the conversion of sinners, and other things*". Our Lady answered saying that some requests would be fulfilled, some not. Then She once again points immediately to the heart of the Message. Why didn't Our Lady fulfil some requests? "*They must amend their lives and ask forgiveness for their sins*". And then, assuming a sadder look, added: "*Do not offend the Lord God anymore, because He is already so much offended*". These words of Our Lady impressed themselves on the hearts of the little shepherd children like a seal, a continual admonition which stayed with them for the whole of their existence: for Jacinta and Francisco that was very short, but longer for Lucia. Such words impressed themselves like fire on their souls. Each time little Jacinta reminded the other two of the importance of offering sacrifices, she remembered that sad face of Our Lady.

Our Lady's sadness

It is essential to focus on two important aspects of this Message: Our Lady with a sad face and God offended by our sins.

When Our Lady appeared to the little shepherd children She was usually surrounded by a beam of light which also emanated from Her hands and the children, immersed in this light, saw themselves reflected in God. That means that Our Lady, since She came from Heaven, from God, brought God's Light and communicated God's Light to these children. She was wrapped in splendour, in beauty, in glory: the Light in fact symbolises the glory of God which surrounds Her; even Her white garment is a symbol of this lucidity of God.

Then to get the children to understand the gravity of the perversity of humanity which continues to offend God, She assumed a sad look. Is the Holy Virgin sad? In Paradise She cannot be sad because She lives in the glory of God; assumed to the Son's right-hand side, She is glorified in Heaven, where there is neither sadness nor suffering. So why does Our Lady of the Rosary reveal Herself with a sad look and with a distressed tone of voice? Her aspect was like a warning to the children and through them to us, too. Of course now Our Lady can no longer suffer and Her face can no longer be sad.

In truth, it is about God's permission to make us "see" that sin really causes offence to God, that we have caused immense sadness to Jesus and Mary at the moment of their lives on earth, when they were expiating our sin, our offences. We remember the words of Jesus: "*Now my soul is troubled, And what should I say – "Father, save me from this hour"? No, it is for this reason that I have come to this hour*" (*Jn* 12:27), and again: "*I am deeply grieved, even to death*" (*Mk* 14:34).

Our Lady was one with Jesus and She, too, in being intimately united with Him, participated in this immense sadness caused by the pain of sin. It was certainly not a sadness manifesting the disorder of the passions. The sadness of Jesus and Mary is caused solely by the pain of seeing themselves offended, by the pain of the ingratitude of men and women. One thinks of the pain a parent feels in seeing him or herself outraged, despised by the child to whom they have given everything: it is an immeasurable pain! If this is true for a parent, how much more it is so for Jesus in seeing Himself maltreated by the ingratitude of men and women: He has given us everything, has offered Himself and is still trampled on by men and women! The blood He sweats in the Passion, His mortal sadness, it was precisely this pain of ingratitude.

Our Lady, assuming this sad look, communicated to the children how both the Passion of Jesus and Her maternal Compassion were really most painful. Her sadness at the time of the apparition was a reference and allusion to the time of Redemption.

It is a serious duty to reflect on our own faults towards God, our own sins, which are an offence against God's goodness, a trampling on His mercy and causing the mortal sadness of Jesus and Mary.

Offence against God

The second aspect of the message concerns God being offended by the faults of men and women. *"Do not offend the Lord our God anymore"*, the Virgin says. What does it mean to say that God is offended? By analogy, one thinks again about a parent who is boorishly offended by one of their children, while that child owes him or her obedience, respect, gratitude and filial piety. Of course here there is a difference between the suffering of a parent and that of God, who is not a man. In God there are no impulses of anger, passionate impulses. In God, precisely because He is God, there is no pain. Pain is a human reality, it is suffered by Jesus in His nature as man. But since Jesus is Son of God, therefore God made man, it can well be said that God suffers, but suffers in Jesus, in His most holy humanity, not in His divinity. Suffering is an imperfection and if God suffered as God, He would no longer be God but one like us. In Himself He is impassive, that is, not subject to the passions, to change, to passing from a state of joy to a state of pain, from a state of joy to one of sadness, and so on, because God is the eternal Love, eternal Perfection, eternal Goodness. If God is impassive and cannot suffer, that does not mean that He is cold and calculating or a mere motor which moves but is not moved. He is Father and precisely because He is Father and uniquely Love, the Good – the supreme Perfection, the supreme Love – in his supreme Goodness feels for us. God's compassion is the free gift of the Son. The Father has sent the Son so that, becoming man, He can suffer and redeem the misery of men and women. God can suffer solely in the Son made man, in the humanity which Jesus has assumed from Mary. Jesus and Mary suffer uniquely during their earthly lives and suffer for our sins.

The offences against Our Lord, all the sins of all times, were all well present during the painful Passion of Jesus and Mary. That is the reason for the terrible suffering of Jesus and Our Lady's redemptive co-participation in the Passion. At that precise moment the Lord saw and redeemed all our sins, even those to be committed in the future. And when men and women, despite such immense redemptive love on the part of the Son of God, continue to sin, it is like saying to God that everything the Son did was in vain, useless. This is really an insult to God; it is the radical reason for the offence caused to God by our sins and the reason why Our Lady exclaimed: "*Do not offend the Lord our God anymore*".

In this sense sin as a continual insult against God fills the chalice of His justice. When the chalice is full it can only overflow and if it overflows the Angel's flaming sword is there to strike against humanity.

So we understand why Our Lady appears with a sad face: She wants to show the children that the offences of men and women sadly continue to fill the chalice of love with so much injustice. Despite God having given everything in the Son, despite Jesus having poured out His Blood for our Redemption, by sinning we state that all this doesn't interest us at all and we continue in our perverse rebellious desires.

This phrase uttered by Our Lady made such a profound impression on the souls of the little shepherd children that they seriously committed themselves to making reparation for the sins committed against God. In every sacrifice offered they remembered: "*Do not offend the Lord our God anymore, because He is already so much offended*".

Justice and Mercy

In relation to what has been said up to now another very important truth can be mentioned: the link between justice and mercy in God. It is a relationship easily misinterpreted today, misunderstood and trivialised in the name of a facile mercy. It is said that God, since He is merciful, would ignore His justice; or better still, God's mercy would put an end to justice, so that the latter is no longer important so as to stop God from carrying out justice, from re-paying sinners with that just payment they merit.

Instead, what is the correct relationship between justice and mercy? These two elements must always remain united, we cannot separate them or even contrast them, as often happens or is preached in good-nature: the God of the Old Testament would be the God of justice, while the God of the New Testament the God of mercy. This is false and what's more is an ancient heresy called "*Marcionism*". Marcion, who lived between the 1st and 2nd centuries (A.D.), believed in fact that there was a dual divinity: an evil God and a good God. The evil God is the avenger of the Old Testament, the good God the merciful one of the New Testament. Christians must feel pardoned by the fact of following the good God and forgetting the evil God. This trap often returns in so much catechesis, when it is said: let's not go back to the Old Testament, where there is a God who punishes, a God who carries out justice. Are there perhaps two divinities fighting each other?

To understand this relationship in a precise and correct manner it is necessary first of all to state that God is one and therefore there is no justice separated from mercy, just as there is no mercy separated from justice. All God's attributes identify with His essence. At the same time it is necessary to see the goal of justice in mercy and the content of mercy in the truth of justice. That means that God is supreme justice, and justice means re-establishing the truth of things, giving to everyone what is due to them, what is merited. A justice without mercy would be almost ferocity, because if God were to give us exactly what we deserve, we would only merit punishment. Instead, since God is Father, "is the Good, the whole Good, the supreme Good" (*Fonti Francescane*, n. 261), His justice is accomplished in His love as Father, therefore is directed to mercy. For its part mercy does not eliminate justice, does not exclude it, but presupposes it and at the same time completes it, because God, in His great love, does not stop at the harshness of justice, but gives us all we need for salvation and therefore uses mercy for us, gives us His love which pardons.

Of course between the Old and the New Testament there is progress, there is a gradual revelation and not an antithesis. God promises salvation and finally gives it in His Son Jesus Christ. In Jesus there is an indissoluble unity between justice and mercy: the Son is given to us to reconcile God's justice. Only the Son of God could repay the enormous injustice caused by our sins. This gift from God is a gift of love, a gift of mercy to us. Therefore judgement belongs to the Son, who came not to condemn but to save us.

While God could not at all close His eyes to evil, because evil is to be condemned, in His eternal goodness He always offers a greater measure, His Love, His mercy.

In concrete terms this means that, if someone rebels against God and *persists* in this offence until the end of their life, obviously that person cannot deserve Paradise, but will deserve what they have chosen, Hell, which Our Lady revealed to the little shepherd children. Saint Thomas says that even in condemning the soul to Hell God is merciful, because He does not punish the damned as much as they would deserve. In a certain sense Hell, too, is an act of God's mercy: it is the truth of the separation for ever of evil from good. To the sinner who converts and desires to live in friendship with God – just like the ungrateful person who nevertheless remains closed in their sin – God will always give this superabundance of mercy up to the last moment of life. The person who is saved, is always saved by an act of God's mercy, but mercy itself will not be able to exclude justice and so Purgatory is necessary, too. Purgatory is a great providence of God, it is an act of His mercy, because through it, while divine justice is accomplished, God gives the possibility once again of purifying us so as to be able to be admitted to His side. It is an act of the highest mercy from this God who wants us with Himself and continually gives us, throughout the whole of life and then in the Hereafter, the possibility of purifying us from the harmful effects of our sins. In this way justice is accomplished in mercy.

This relationship between God's justice and mercy is very important so as to trivialise neither one nor the other. Reference could be made to the Saint of Divine Mercy, Saint Faustina Kowalska: Jesus would not let her believe that His mercy excludes justice and closes Hell. She, too, saw the tremendous reality of Hell! Why did Jesus ask her to bring the message of mercy to humanity? To make people aware of the possibility of eternal perdition.

Finally, it is necessary to add that there is experience of God's great mercy in confession. Confession extends, so to speak, the Passion of Jesus, because it administers to the penitent the Blood of Jesus Christ. Every time we confess our owns sins we are washed in the Blood of Jesus Christ. There is effectively the manifestation of a justice which is accomplished in the emanation of the Blood of Christ, in the remission of sins which is abundance of God's mercy. Each time we approach this Sacrament in a repentant manner, we can receive God's forgiveness, even if we have committed the most serious crimes before God: if we are repentant, God forgives. Is this not a manifestation of His mercy?

Mercy does not exclude the Passion of Jesus, in fact, it derives from the Passion, from the Blood of Jesus. Otherwise by what would our sins be washed away? By what would they be forgiven? Who would be able to forgive our sins? Certainly not the beautiful words of this or that preacher, but solely the Blood of Jesus Christ. That is why Saint Pio repeatedly said that the Blood of Christ is administered in the sacrament of Confession. In confession we see the profound unity between justice and mercy. Justice is what Jesus has done for us, what He has paid for us. In confession that great treasure acquired by Him ransoms us once again from the state of misery and with a pouring out of goodness, of love for our salvation, God bestows His forgiveness.

If, instead, it was said that God's mercy is so great that by now there is no longer any need to take the trouble to live in God's grace and to renounce one's own sin, it would be saying that Jesus in the end did nothing for us, it would be like transforming confession into a psychological session, which is not being saved. If this profound link between justice and mercy is not borne well in mind, there is the risk of thwarting what Jesus has done for us.

There must be necessarily a "limit" to evil – Hell as merciful justice – and a pouring out of mercy which completes justice eternally – Paradise – to understand the reality of the Love which pardons and the misery of the people who instead can resist it. Only the supernatural truth of eternal salvation and eternal perdition can definitively balance this justice-mercy couple. Otherwise, everything would be reduced to pure moralism.

Fatima: the whole of Faith

It is important to remember that Faith is a well-connected whole of all the truths revealed by God, so that if you challenge even just one element, like mercy, or justice, gradually the whole edifice crumbles, Faith empties and believing no longer has any meaning. Faith becomes a "do-it-yourself".

So, for example, by exaggerating (or diluting) the truth of mercy you reach the point of demolishing completely the supernatural reality of Redemption, therefore of the Sacraments and in particular the Eucharist and Penance. If the Redemption of Jesus is no longer the offering of Christ and of His Blood for our eternal salvation, because, essentially, there is the "mercy which covers everything", then, consequently – one of the many consequences – the Eucharist is no longer the Body of Christ, it is no longer the Body of the One who gave Himself for us. What will the Eucharist be? A memory of Jesus, as sadly happens, a symbol of love. What will Confession be? A psychological dialogue. That is why so many people say there is no need to confess so often, that once in a while is enough, or else it is sufficient to have a dialogue with the priest who perhaps will offer a word of comfort.

Fatima helps to meditate on these truths of our Faith and to see them as a good harmonious whole, a whole which must be respected just as it is, according to the Catechism of the Church. If you read the Catechism and the Message of Fatima this complementarity reveals itself and at the same time the Message of Fatima reflects on the beauty and harmony of our Faith: it is a reminder of those unavoidable, most important truths which cannot be forgotten. That is the most profound content of this expression of the Holy Virgin: "*Do not offend the Lord our God anymore, because He is already so much offended*".

These words evoke what happened in such a predominant manner: men and women and "enlightened" Catholics continue to offend the Lord justifying sin and offences against God with so many quibbles. So many theological formulae have been drawn up to say that essentially men and women cannot liberate themselves from their sinful condition. Men and women sin and can continue to do so as long as they in some way entrust themselves to mercy. Luther would open the path to this deviation. It is rather God and the Gospel who must adapt to the historical condition of wounded humanity. Acceptance of human misery will lead to compromising the truths of Faith and an unorthodox Faith will lead to living in an immoral world. It is going backwards, not forward.

But challenging the truths of Faith, especially the last truths about which Fatima reminds us – salvation, perdition, justice, mercy, sin – is returning to the reality as it was before Christianity, that is, to idolatry, to being simply material people. Because, as the Fathers would explain, the gods were simply projections of the passions of men and women. Hence the responsibility to which Our Lady recalls us in the Message of Fatima, responsibility and commitment which we now can summarise in the following points:

a) the request by Our Lady to take seriously one's own Christian vocation, which consists in making ourselves new creatures in Jesus, by virtue of His Redemption, and so to live as true children of God, in His grace;

b) at work in the world is a *"mystery of lawlessness"* (cf. *2 Thess* 2:7), as Saint Paul would say, which is raging in the world, sin continues to claim victims and lead many to perdition, because they are seduced by the evil reality of sin;

c) however God is mercy and love, He desires the salvation of men and women and so provides a remedy: the Immaculate Heart of Mary.

The Immaculate Heart of Mary asks the Holy children, and therefore each of us, to be collaborators in the salvation of souls. How?

- by a life of authentic faith in the God One and Three;

- by a life of adoration of God;

-   by a life of hope and charity;

-   by the offering of ourselves for the conversion of sinners.

So in the Message of Fatima the following are absolutely central: prayer, therefore adoration of God, and sacrifice. Sister Lucia often asked herself: "*How must we sacrifice ourselves?*" That explains when, towards the 80s, she took up again the Message of Fatima to write what had matured in her now long meditation:

> "*What was Our Lady asking us when she asked to offer sacrifices? She was asking us first of all to offer the main sacrifice, detachment from sin, from the surrender to vices, from the surrender to wild passions. The very first sacrifice is the rejection of sin. Then all the other sacrifices, all that we can offer with a supernatural spirit, like renunciation, like penance for the salvation of souls. And praying this continually: "My God, it is for Your love, for the conversion of sinners, in reparation for the sins committed against the Immaculate Heart of Mary"*"

The "sins committed against the Immaculate Heart of Mary"

Finally, there is another detail: "*Oh Jesus, it is for Your love...*": Our Lady teaches the children to recite this prayer when offering a sacrifice. Love! It is this which seasons the sacrifice with prayer and also joy: when it is done for love of God. At Fatima Our Lady did not ask for us to be masochistic, to love pain for pain's sake, to harm ourselves in order to do something good for God. No. She asks simply for a greater love, She asks that we love God and demonstrate it by these renunciations and in reparation for all the sins committed against the Immaculate Heart of Mary. When subsequently the Most Holy Virgin appeared to Sister Lucia, now in a monastery, to ask her for the "Five First Saturdays of the month", She showed her Her Heart pierced by thorns, using this other image to underline more intensely the reason for Her requests for reparation. The prayer always echoed in Lucia's soul:

> *"O Jesus, it is for Your love, for the conversion of sinners, and in reparation for the sins done against the Immaculate Heart of Mary".*

All the sins are like thorns thrust into Our Lady's Heart. Must we say that all the sins committed against God reverberate in the Heart of Mary? Yes, of course. That most pure, immaculate Heart is the Heart of the Mother of God. The sins committed against the Son are necessarily also sins against the Mother, therefore thorns for Her Heart.

We can even say that the pain of the Immaculate Heart is more acute than that which afflicts the Heart of Jesus, because in Her Heart as Mother all the sins reverberate in a much, much more acute manner. The Message of Fatima is summarised in this prayer of reparation. To make reparation for the sins committed against the Heart of Our Lady means making reparation for the sins committed against Jesus, because between Jesus and Mary there is a most profound union: they are mother and son.

"Do not offend the Lord our God anymore, because He is already so much offended". With these words the Lady dressed in White disappeared and the apparition of 13 October ended then with that incredible sign from heaven: after a night of torrential rain – by now the whole of Cova da Iria had become a great puddle – suddenly the sun dried everyone and began to spin, to dance in the sky, to the point that many people were frightened. Other miracles immediately followed on from this one, other prodigious cures which happened on the same day. The miracle – then others – attested to the ultimate guarantee of the supernatural truthfulness of this Message.

JACINTA, "LILY OF CANDOUR" AND "SHINING PEARL"

At this point of our itinerary in the footsteps of the little shepherd children, to affirm the profound spirituality of the Message of Fatima we will focus on the figures of the two little shepherd saints, Francisco and Jacinta, two little mystics, two giants of holiness. To examine in depth the figures of the little shepherd children is very useful, because in them lives the charism of the apparitions, being bearers of this Message; consequently, the example of their lives is of great value in verifying its supernatural truthfulness. For this reason the Bishop of Leiria commissioned Lucia to recall all her memories in the *Memoirs*.

We begin this new more hagiographic path with Jacinta. According to Lucia and Francisco, too, Saint Jacinta was "an angel of God". Whoever knew her wanted so much to speak to her, to be in her presence, even if it cost her a great deal, especially when she became ill. Everyone confessed that they felt a great grace being close to her, because she really was a child of God. She was described as a "little mystic".

A fuller and very beautiful picture of this little visionary, Saint Jacinta Marto, can be deduced by reading the various testimonies, especially the main ones which are the *Memoirs* of Sister Lucia. And in particular the *First Memoir*, written in December 1935, the richest in terms of information about the Message and the little shepherd children, especially Saint Jacinta.

What is eternity?

Some of Lucia's testimonies deal a lot with the holiness and great desire which always animated little Jacinta to offer herself in sacrifice for sinners. How come the desire to offer was so much alive in Jacinta? Because, as Lucia recalled in her *Third Memoir*, written in 1942, where she went into the content of the Secret in depth, the vision of Hell impressed itself so intensely on the heart of Jacinta like a warning, for which she felt she had a very serious responsibility; she often thought of the great suffering of the damned, and so fathomed evermore the value of Our Lady's request to offer sacrifices.

One of the main meditations of this child concerned eternity. She often dwelt on this meditation and when she thought of the eternity of perdition, she lost her way, she was no longer able to understand the dimension of it. When she reasoned about eternity, she then reached the fear of thinking about the suffering of the damned, the fact that these souls are condemned eternally in this place.

Lucia recalled that after the vision of Hell, Jacinta literally changed. Often she sat thoughtfully on a rock and no longer wanted to play. When Lucia and Francisco asked her *"Jacinta, come and play"*, she replied: *"I don't want to play today"*. *"Why not?"* *"Because I'm thinking"*.

In the Lisbon hospital , where she then died in 1920, Jacinta herself confessed that – as reported by her godmother, who was superior of the Sisters in the hospital – *"I love to think"*. In fact she was a child who was concentrated in meditation and was very quiet. Thinking meant for her meditating on the words of the Lady in White. She said:

> *"That Lady told us to say the Rosary and to make sacrifices for the conversion of sinners. So from now on, when we say the Rosary we must say the whole Hail Mary and the whole Our Father!"*

Yes, because initially they only said : "Ave Maria, Santa Maria". They had contrived this shortcut to hurry things up and then go and play! A little like we do, wanting to end praying immediately to then do other things.

One day Jacinta, seated on her rock, thoughtful, asked Lucia: *"That Lady also said that many souls go to hell! What is hell, then?"*. Lucia replied:

"It's like a big deep pit of wild beasts, with an enormous fire in it – that's how my mother used to explain it to me – and that's where people go who commit sins and don't confess them. They stay there and burn for ever!"

Jacinta then continued: *"And they never get out of there again?"* *"No!"*, said Lucia. *"Not even after many, many years?"* she asked again.

"No; hell never ends. And heaven never ends either. Whoever goes to heaven, never leaves it again. And whoever goes to hell, never leaves it either. They're eternal, don't you see! They never end", added Lucia.

When this child understood that Hell and Heaven are eternal, she began to think about eternity. What is eternity? It is a dimension beyond time, which neither begins nor ends, has no limits. *"That was how, for the first time"*, wrote Lucia, *"we made a meditation on hell and eternity"*. That was while they were putting the flocks out to pasture. Lucia provides us with this interesting detail:

"What made the biggest impression on Jacinta was the idea of eternity. Even in the middle of a game, she would stop and ask: 'But listen! Doesn't hell end after many, many years, then?' or again: 'Those people burning in hell, don't they ever die? And don't they turn into ashes? And if people pray very much for sinners, won't Our Lord get them out of there? And if they make sacrifices as well? Poor sinners! We have to pray and make many sacrifices for them!' Then she went on: 'How good that Lady is! She has already promised to take us to heaven!'"

Jacinta's favourite loves

Jacinta had essentially three favourite "loves":

a) love of sinners;

b) love of the Holy Father, of whom she would have a special vision;

c) love of the Immaculate Heart of Mary.

These were always the three aims which were intended in the offering of sacrifices.

Love of sinners

She invented so many sacrifices for her love of sinners. For example, she had decided to give her snack to the sheep and to eat the acorns from the oak trees instead. *"Jacinta!"*, Lucia said to her one day, *"don't eat that; it's too bitter!"*. *"But it's because it's bitter that I'm eating it, for the conversion of sinners"*. All three children made a pact: every time they met poor people, they would give them their lunch, while they would feed on acorns. Lucia says: *"Jacinta's thirst for making sacrifices seemed insatiable"*. In fact, as she later confessed on her deathbed, a great love burned in her heart and so she could not but offer sacrifices, could not but make sacrifices for the conversion of sinners:

> *"Oh, if I could only put in the heart of everyone in the world the fire that is burning in me and makes me love so much the Heart of Jesus and the Heart of Mary"*, she exclaimed.

The vision of Hell made a very strong impression on Jacinta. When she spoke about it with the other two, she said:

> *"Oh, Hell! Hell! How sorry I am for the souls who go to hell! And the people down there, burning alive, like wood*

in the fire!" Then, shuddering, she knelt down with her hands joined, and recited the prayer that Our Lady had taught us: 'Oh my Jesus! Forgive us, save us from the fire of hell. Lead all souls to heaven, especially those who are most in need'".

Often she said to Francisco:

"Francisco! Francisco! Are you praying with me? We must pray very much, to save souls from hell! So many go there! So many!"

Then in her simplicity she asked:

"Why doesn't Our Lady show hell to sinners? If they saw it, they would not sin, so as to avoid going there! You must tell Our Lady to show hell to all the people (referring to those who were in the Cova da Iria at the time of the Apparition). You'll see how they will be converted".

However, the vision of Hell to the three little children had been a special grace. Lucia herself recognised, when she wrote her *Memoirs*, that Jacinta let herself be filled by such a spirit of mortification and penance that "*God willed to bestow on her a special grace of God, through the Immaculate Heart of Mary*" especially [because] "*she had looked upon hell, and had seen the ruin of souls who fall therein*". It is a grace which Our Lady granted to these children by a special preference, so that in turn they might become messengers of this truth. What Lucia adds is very interesting:

"Some people, even the most devout, refuse to speak to children about hell, in case it would frighten them. Yet God did not hesitate to show hell to three children, one of whom was only six years old, knowing well that they would be horrified to the point of, I would almost dare to say, withering away with fear".

Our Lady was not afraid to reveal a similar reality to three little children. It is a grace because through their witness so many can renew their faith and change their lives.

Also of interest is a dialogue between Saint Jacinta and Lucia, in which the little Jacinta poses various questions to Lucia, who was older and was a bit like their teacher:

> "*What are the sins people commit, for which they go to hell?' 'I don't know! Perhaps the sin of not going to Mass on Sunday, of stealing, of saying ugly words, of cursing and of swearing'. 'So for just one word, then, people can go to hell?' 'Well, it's a sin!' 'It wouldn't be hard for them to keep quiet, and to go to Mass! I'm so sorry for sinners! If only I could show them hell!' Suddenly, she would seize hold of me and say: 'I'm going to heaven, but you are staying here. If Our Lady lets you, tell everybody what hell is like, so that they won't commit any more sins and not go to hell*".

Such love for sinners, such charity! She knew she had been chosen by Our Lady as a messenger of this truth for others, so she could not be consoled, she wanted to do everything so that sinners might understand the gravity of sin and letting themselves commit evil; so she always wanted to offer sacrifice, mortification. When Lucia said: "*Listen, Jacinta! Come and eat now*", she replied: "*No! I'm offering this sacrifice for sinners who eat too much*"; or, when she was already ill, Lucia went to Mass and said: "*Jacinta, don't come! You can't, you're not able. Besides, today is not a Sunday!*", but she replied: "*That doesn't matter! I'm going for sinners who don't go on a Sunday*". If, then, she happened to hear someone swear, she covered her face with her hands and said:

> "*Oh, my God, don't those people realize that they can go to hell for saying those things? My Jesus, forgive them and convert them. They certainly don't know that they are offending God by all this! What a pity, my Jesus! I'll pray for them*".

Love of the Holy Father

Her other great love was the Holy Father. Jacinta "fell in love" with the Holy Father when she had the vision of the third part of the Secret. Our Lady had said: "*The Holy Father will have much to suffer*", but the little shepherd children didn't know who the "Holy Father" was.

In her *Third Memoir*, Lucia recounts that Jacinta had another vision of the Pope. One day the three little children went to pass the time of their siesta by the Marto family's well. Jacinta sat on the stone slabs on top of the well, while Francisco went with Lucia to look for some wild honey among the brambles. After a while Jacinta called Lucia:

> "*'Didn't you see the Holy Father?' 'No'. 'I don't know how it was'*", said Jacinta, "*but I saw the Holy Father in a very big house, kneeling by a table, with his head buried in his hands, and he was weeping. Outside the house, there were many people. Some of them were throwing stones, others were cursing him and using bad language. Poor Holy Father, we must pray very much for him*".

Jacinta recalled the words of the Most Holy Virgin: if sinners did not stop offending God, a war worse than the one already on-going would break out and the Pope would have much to suffer.

That vision of the "Bishop dressed in white", with tears on his face, was a new great warning for her. From then on, every time she offered her sacrifices to God, she always added: "*and for the Holy Father*", just as at the end of saying the Rosary, she always said three *Ave Maria* for him. Once she said: "*How I'd love to see the Holy Father! So many people come here, but the Holy Father never does*". In her innocence, she thought that the Supreme Pontiff could visit there like any other pilgrim. Is this not a clear evangelical sign of the little one's greatness?

Love for the Immaculate Heart of Mary

Saint Jacinta then had particular love for the Immaculate Heart of Mary. Our Lady had said to the little shepherd children that She would soon bring them to Heaven, but they had to suffer a great deal. In fact, sometime after the apparition, in 1918-1919, Francisco and Jacinta became seriously ill due to *"Spanish flu"* and little Jacinta had a very strong festering pleurisy which consumed her and soon led to her death. Francisco died in 1919 and she in 1920.

Jacinta was admitted to hospital twice, first in Ourém in 1919 and then to the hospital where she died, in Lisbon. When she left for Lisbon, she left alone, because her mother was unable to follow her. How painful it must have been for such a small child to find herself alone! And after the death of Francisco, Our Lady asked her for another great sacrifice, that of dying alone, without even Lucia, whom she would not see again; without Francisco, to whom she was very attached, and no longer with the comfort of her mother. She would die alone! What despair it could have caused to a small child to know that she would die from such a terrible illness and, furthermore, alone! Instead, even though she was suffering terribly, Jacinta accepted everything through love of the Immaculate Heart of Mary.

Even knowing that she would die and would have to suffer a great deal, she said: *"It will not be long now before I go to heaven"*. And speaking to Lucia:

> *"You will remain here to make known that God wishes to establish in the world devotion to the Immaculate Heart of Mary. When you are to say this, don't go and hide. Tell everybody that God grants us graces through the Immaculate Heart of Mary; that people are to ask her for them; and that the Heart of Jesus wants the Immaculate Heart of Mary to be venerated at His side. Tell them also to pray to the Immaculate Heart of Mary for peace, since God has entrusted it to her. If I could only put into the*

hearts of all, the fire that is burning within my own heart, and that makes me love the Hearts of Jesus and Mary so very much!"

These final words should be carefully noted. Love of the Hearts of Jesus and Mary stimulated her to a continual offering. The reparatory offering can never be separated from love for the Hearts of Jesus and Mary. It is charity which nourishes the offering and if there is no offering, it is a sign that charity is missing. When, as often happens today, there is a desire to love God and one's neighbour without the offering of sacrifice, that implies that that love is not a love-charity, but a love-sentiment, a human love. Charity leads to a becoming one with God, because God is charity. And whoever loves with God's charity, loves as God loves. And how does God love? *"For God so loved the world that he gave his only Son"* (*Jn* 3:16). That is how one loves: with the gift of self, with self-sacrifice. And how has Jesus loved? *"Having loved his own who were in the world, he loved them to the end"* (*Jn* 13:1), in other words, to death on the Cross, to the gift of Eucharist.

Sometimes we are tempted to think that the little shepherd children exaggerated a little. It can in fact happen that, having meditated for a long time on the marvels of Fatima, one quickly sets everything aside thinking that, in the end, it is an exaggeration, a completely childish commotion. If you then hear some preaching, some thought, you're convinced. The enemy, as well as self-love and weakness, whispers in the ear that Fatima is an exaggeration, that God does not want this, that He is satisfied with much simpler things. It is important to love God! Of course. But how does that love manifest itself? God has *given*, that is, has *offered* for us His Son: that is love.

The little shepherd children teach us what loving God really means, especially Jacinta with her continual desire of offering; it is the little-great mystic who loves Jesus with a "burning within her heart". Love of sinners, of the Holy Father and of the Immaculate Heart of Mary constitute the precious inheritance of love, reparation, supplication which Jacinta gives to us.

In 1919 Jacinta went into hospital and began what was for her a real Calvary. Having reached the point where she could no longer ingest any food, she was finding it difficult to swallow, but offered everything *"for the love of our Good God and of the Immaculate Heart of Mary, for sinners and for the Holy Father"*.

Our Lady's confidant

In hospital Our Lady appeared to her a number of times, confiding in her many things which she reported to her godmother. These were very profound thoughts, which such a small child would certainly not have been able to invent. She said that these teachings were imparted to her *"by Our Lady, but I think some things. I like to think!"*

Jacinta makes her love that of the Immaculate Heart of Mary. From this union between the words said by Our Lady and her personal reflections a beautiful work has emerged: notes of Jacinta's final days which Fr Fonseca – one of the greatest historians of Fatima – drew above all from the *Memoirs* of Sister Lucia and from the memories of the godmother who assisted Jacinta in hospital and transcribed what she told her.

For example, Jacinta said: *"The sins that send most souls to hell are sins of impurity"*. She saw that the most frequent sin was impurity; and added: *"Fashions that will greatly offend Our Lord will appear"*. Hasn't all that happened, in fact? Today there are horrifying fashions; some people try to undress more than dress and thus reveal their own bodies. A naked, vulnerable, empty body.

At the basis of all these degrading fashions lies the idea that the person is simply appearance. But this brings with it significant harm: in fact, when people limit themselves to living by appearance, even more pernicious problems open up as a consequence of the terrible separation between body and spirit. Starting out from this philosophy one reaches, for example, deciding when to die: the human person is only desire, spirit. So everyone can decide what they want to be sexually. Supporting this materialist ideology destroys the person. Everything is justified by freedom: I am free to live, I am free to die, to create family as I want.

These fashions have come and offend God. Fashions which are a manifestation of a way of life contrary to God's Law. Then there are those who undress to then dress themselves in tattoos. The philosophy of the tattoo has tribal origins, where people distinguish themselves not by who they are but by the signs on the body. Today many young people do it to "embellish" the body. All those who do it have a thought which lumps them all together: the philosophy at the basis of this phenomenon consists in the need for something distinctive (in common) for people to show themselves off, because people of our time no longer know how to identify themselves: being distant from God, they seek another way to recognise themselves; they are no longer children of God but belong to a new group, often understood in a tribal manner. *"The Church has no fashions. Our Lord is always the same"*, retorted Jacinta.

The little shepherdess also spoke about wars, saying they are punishment for the sins of humanity:

> *"The sins of the world are very great. Our Lady has said that there is much war and discord in the world: wars are nothing but punishments for the sins of the world. Our Lady can no longer hold back the arm of her beloved Son from the world"* .

God always punishes us for our good. God only does good. Our good is salvation. In view of this good, He can want a punishment for our conversion, recalling us to eternal realities through a tragedy, a war. The punished soul is always loved by God by virtue of the fact that God created it. God knows everything and directs everything to a good end which is Providence. Even if He allows war, it is to punish the sins of men and women. The Holy Virgin also said it in the third apparition: if people convert, if they do penance, God will yet pardon; but if they do not change their lives, He *"[will] punish the world for its crimes, by means of war..."* as a punishment. To punish means making pure, to purify.

Teachings from hospital

We have said that Jacinta was the confidant of Our Lady even in the final moments of her life. Sometimes her godmother who helped her would sit at her feet and the little one would say: *"Please move aside for Our Lady stood there"*. That clearly revealed that she had other visions of the Holy Virgin, who assisted her in her illness.

Returning to the precious legacy left to us by Jacinta, through the work of the collection by her godmother, let us try in brief to summarise the content of those thoughts referred to above and see them in their unity.

a) The sins that send most souls to hell are sins of impurity.

b) She then talks about the scandalous fashions which will offend God; something which is contrary to the Church, which does not have fashions.

c) The sins of the world are very great and deserve punishment. Our Lady Herself can no longer hold back the arm of Her beloved Son from the world.

d) It is necessary to do penance: if men and women repent, the Lord will yet pardon, but if they do not change their lives the punishment will be inevitable. It is not possible to understand exactly what Jacinta meant, but there is the perception of another great punishment, as she confided in her godmother.

It is important to remember that if people convert and change their lives, the punishment will end. Sometimes men and women are so stubborn that they close themselves to God and no longer hear His voice which is admonishing, they become deaf to every supernatural call; then the Lord uses these means, too, sometimes very painful, precisely to shake this spiritual lethargy. If people do penance and change lives the punishment can also cease.

In these revelations, too, as already in the apparitions, the Immaculate revealed Herself to be sad. Hence little Jacinta replied: "*Poor Our Lady! Our Lady pains me so much! It pains me so much!*"

e)   The meditation on eternity is very important. Another of Jacinta's great phrases was: "*If people knew what eternity is, they would do everything to change their lives*".

We have seen that she loved meditation, thinking very much, a characteristic which fascinated Francisco, too, closely linked to prayer, especially hidden prayer. Her motto was: "*To pray and make reparation to console Jesus and Mary*".

Our Lady said that the reason why so many souls went to hell was because they did not think about eternal life, about the afterlife, and so they set out in a too casual manner towards eternity, which will not be the same for everyone. Sometimes, as happened to the little shepherdess, in the attempt to think of eternity one is struck by confusion, because eternity is a present which remains, a present identical to itself. It is not a succession of moments, of hours, of days. Paradise is actuality, the present of the infinite love of God. Hell is the actuality of the hatred, of the hostility towards God, of rebellion, of distancing from Him.

When one speaks about the eschatological realities, the last things such as Hell and Paradise, it must be understood that it is about a new, eternal condition, a being in this new dimension, which is no longer that of space, of the succession of minutes, of days, of experiences, but is a remaining forever in a today which never fades. The measure of this "remaining" is eternity, in other words a non-measure.

Hence little Jacinta asked Lucia: "*And [people] never get out of there again? ... Not even after many, many years?*" But a thousand years are like just a day before God, says the Sacred Scriptures, and a day is like a thousand years (cf. *2 Pet* 3:8).

If we meditate a little more on the eternal length of these eschatological conditions, we cannot but mend our ways: "*If people knew what eternity is* – that is, this new, definitive condition, from which you cannot get out, you cannot change, said Jacinta – *then they would certainly do penance for their sins*".

Also of interest were some expressions of Jacinta which do not require any comment:

f) "Doctors do not know how to treat their patients because they have no love for God";

g) "If the government left the Church in peace and gave liberty to our holy religion, they would be blessed by God";

h) She added, speaking to her godmother, who was a nun: "My good godmother, pray much for sinners! Pray much for priests! Pray much for religious! Pray much for those who govern!"

A wider field of action: the Church, the world

Such was the spiritual maturity acquired by this child; from when she was little, happy-go-lucky, she loved to play, but after the visions of Our Lady and the experience of the years of suffering she began to feel on herself the whole responsibility for the Church, for humanity, for those who govern; she acquired a much broader vision of life. This is an important element. A supernatural factor transformed the lives of these children and made them capable of becoming instruments of a message given to the whole of humanity. Therefore this child felt responsible also for priests, the religious, those who govern, all sinners: she had a broadened outlook over humanity.

Fatima is a message of hope for the whole of humanity. Once someone knows about the Fatima-event they can no longer just think about themselves and their own salvation, their own family, their own work. Fatima teaches about growing spiritually, striving ever higher, to go beyond oneself to broaden intelligence, the heart, to the needs of the Church, of humanity, to the sad tragedy of people who sadly ignore God, who do not want to love Him and thus set out towards perdition.

Since the Lord is the Creator of the universe, of heaven, of the earth and every human being, when He enters into our life He asks us to be bearers of a responsibility for the good of humanity. This is supernatural charity, love of souls, of all people to be saved. Like the little shepherd children, each of us must commit ourselves to spiritual progress which is responsibility for the world. My sanctification is a good for all, for many. Clearly each person has their problems, their own crosses, and has to ask for graces for themselves. But that is not sufficient. It must be understood that Our Lady, through us, wants to reach those who are furthest away. That radiates in the life of Saint Jacinta, who at just 9 years of age took upon herself the problems and needs of everyone, especially the priests, for whom she had very, very strong words, which evidently must have been suggested to her by the Most Holy Virgin, since she did not know any other priests other than her parish priest. Here are those words:

i) *"Priests should only occupy themselves with the affairs of the Church. Priests should be pure, very pure. The disobedience of priests and religious to their superiors and to the Holy Father greatly offends Our Lord"*.

How was this little child able to think of the disobedience of the religious and priests to the Holy Father? A child of 9 years old does not have these problems! Spiritual maturity made her understand these much more profound problems, which are the problems of our Church today, often problems of infidelity to the priestly vocation.

Then Jacinta spoke once again to her godmother, saying:

j) *"Dear godmother, do not walk in the midst of luxury. Flee from riches. Be very fond of holy poverty and silence. Have much charity even for those who are bad. Speak ill of no one and flee from those who do so. Be very patient, for patience leads us to heaven".*

This advice is applicable to everyone. There is a need for charity towards annoying people. Charity forces us to try and treat annoying people as if they were our best friend.

k) *"Speak ill of no one and flee from those who do so"*. This is about bad language.

There is a need for a careful examination of conscience, because the tongue does not let itself be controlled easily and sometimes takes us where we would rather not be.

Some do nothing but talk. Thus says Saint James in his letter: "The tongue is the rudder of our life" (cf. *Jas* 3), in other words, we go where our speech leads us. If the tongue is aimed at the contempt of others, the whole of life is orientated in that direction, life itself gets dirty, is soiled! There is a need to be very careful so as not to waste the time which the Lord still gives us to speak badly, instead use it to speak well, to always seek to speak well of one's brothers and sisters.

Here we come back to that fundamental element revealed by Jacinta, which is meditation on eternity. If we think that eternity will never end while the time we have here will end, but is directed to bringing us to eternity, then the need not to lose time can be understood, because the time available is really limited compared to eternity without end and every moment is precious for earning eternity; it is here, in time, that one's own eternity is decided!

Jacinta continued speaking to her godmother:

1) "*Be very patient, for patience leads us to heaven. Mortification and sacrifices greatly please Our Lord. I would enter a convent with great joy but my joy is greater because I am going to Heaven. To be a religious, one has to be very pure in soul and in body*".
And the godmother asked:

> "*Do you know what it means to be pure?*" "*I do, I do. To be pure in body is to keep chastity. To be pure in soul is not to commit sins, not to look at what one should not see, not to steal, never to lie, always to tell the truth however hard it may be*". "*But who taught you these things? This wisdom you have is a wisdom which is not yours*". Jacinta replied to her: "*Our Lady. Some things, but I think them, because I like thinking*".

She was a child enlightened by divine wisdom. She desired to go to a convent, but she desired Paradise even more. Instead something else saddened her a little: she wanted her two sisters to become nuns, while her mother did not agree. One day Jacinta's mother, Olímpia de Jesus, went to visit her daughter and the superior asked her if she would be happy if Jacinta's two other sisters were to become nuns. The good mother replied: "*God save me!*" The little Saint was saddened and said: "*Mother does not want my sisters to become nuns. Our Lady will soon take them to Heaven*". In fact, they died very soon, shortly after Jacinta.

Heaven opens...

So little Jacinta moved towards her death. On 2 February 1920 she confessed, received communion and knew she was about to go back into hospital for the final phase of her illness which would lead to her death. Before going there, she went to take her leave of her "hidden Jesus" in the Tabernacle.

She suffered greatly during the period of her illness, and yet she never complained, always imploring Our Lady with that formula of offering her illness, her sacrifice. She said: *"Patience! We must all suffer to get to Heaven"*; *"O Jesus, all for love of you and for the conversion of sinners"*. Then, almost in the last moments of her life, she said to her godmother: *"I am not complaining anymore. Our Lady has appeared again and said that She was coming soon to bring me to Heaven"*.

On Friday 20 February she made her last confession and asked that she be brought the holy Viaticum. About 10.30 p.m. that same day Our Lady came to take her and bring her to Heaven. She was 10 years old: this little flower was gently uprooted to blossom in God's garden.

Jacinta, this 10 year-old child, teaches us many things, but perhaps the most beautiful teaching by which she exhorts us is that of preferring these loves: love of the sinners to be saved; love of the Holy Father, the "Bishop dressed in white" whom when she understood it was the Vicar of Christ on earth loved with great simplicity; love of the Immaculate Heart of Mary; and finally love of the priests and the religious, who *"must be pure, very pure"*. Loving the Immaculate Heart, Jacinta guarded every other love in that pure Heart. In the Virgin Mary, Jacinta became a most pure rose which intoxicated our earthly homeland by its smell, showing to us the way to Heaven.

FRANCISCO, THE LITTLE SHEPHERD OF THE "HIDDEN JESUS"

After Jacinta we now focus on Francisco. Little Francisco Marto, brother of Jacinta and little cousin of Lucia, was born in

1908. He was of a peaceful and submissive disposition. He was not capricious, he loved to play his pipe rather than dance like his little sister. Often he went up to his mountains to admire the sunrise or sunset, which reminded him of the Lord more stunning than any other oil lamp. He played his pipe and sang and thus loved to spend his time while the flocks were at pasture.

Unlike the other two Fatima visionaries, Francisco saw the apparition of the Angel but did not hear the words. So he insistently asked what the Angel had said. He often thought of the Angel.

Lucia told him everything that the heavenly Messenger had said in the first and second apparitions, but it seems that he still did not understand and asked: *"Who is the Most High? What is the meaning of 'The Hearts of Jesus and Mary are attentive to the voice of your supplications?'"* Then he paused to reflect more intensely on that angelic message. That was rather a clear indication of his more meditative nature. During the third apparition, from the angelic hands the children received Holy Communion, from which fell drops of Blood which then rested on the chalice beneath. Once the first few days were over after that unique experience, Francisco, still amazed by what had happened, asked Lucia:

> *"The Angel gave you Holy Communion, but what was it that he gave to Jacinta and me?" "It was Holy Communion, too", replied Jacinta, with inexpressible joy. "Didn't you see that it was the Blood that fell from the Host?" "I felt that God was within me, but I didn't know how!", added Francisco. Then, prostrating on the ground, he and his sister remained for a long time, saying over and over again the prayer of the Angel 'Most Holy Trinity...'"*

Rosaries and sacrifices for Heaven

With the first apparition of Our Lady in May 1917 Francisco changed a great deal in his attitude. He became more reflective, he wanted to do everything to give joy to God. He often lingered in silence contemplating the pain of the Heart of Jesus and of the Immaculate Heart of Mary, so offended by so many sins. During the first apparition Francisco did not see Our Lady and did not even hear Her message, it was reported to him by Lucia and Jacinta. The words addressed directly to him by the Holy Virgin: *"He [Francisco] will go there [Heaven] too, but he must say many Rosaries"*, worried him especially as soon as he heard them from Lucia and Jacinta. He was very happy about the certainty of going to Heaven, but wanted to pray many Rosaries so as not to lose that certainty, especially to ensure that many other souls went there with him, too. From then he was committed with all his strength to say many Rosaries: *"Oh my dear Our Lady! I'll say as many rosaries as you want!"*

At the start of the May apparition Our Lady presented Herself as the One who came from Heaven. That Lady all dressed in White brought with Her, in Her purity and Her incomparable beauty, a longing for Heaven which so inflamed the hope of the little shepherd children. Thus wrote Lucia in her *Memoir* devoted to her cousin Francisco:

> *"And from then on, he made a habit of moving away from us, as though going for a walk. When we called him and asked him what he was doing, he raised his hand and showed me his rosary. If we told him to come and play, and say the rosary with us afterwards, he replied: 'I'll pray then as well. Don't you remember that Our Lady said I must pray many rosaries?'*
> *He said to me on one occasion: 'I loved seeing the Angel, but I loved still more seeing Our Lady. What I loved most of all was to see Our Lord in that light from Our Lady which penetrated our hearts. I love God so much! But He is very sad because of so many sins! We must never commit any sins again'".*

Francisco accepted every sort of sacrifice so as not to lose the blessed Homeland. He was faithful to the promise which the visionaries made not to say anything to the parents about the apparition of the Lady in White. Jacinta, the youngest, was unable to hold out, but Francisco remained firm. So as not to lie, however, he had to confirm to the parents that what Jacinta had confided to them was true. A "small persecution" broke out: the little shepherd children became the object of threats, exhausting interrogation, but offered everything with great peace, conscious of the heavenly promise. Francisco reassured Jacinta and Lucia with these words:

> *"Our Lady told us that we would have much to suffer, but I don't mind. I'll suffer all that She wishes! What I want is to go to heaven".*

In Our Lady's second apparition, Francisco was very struck by the revelation of the Immaculate Heart of Mary as refuge and path which would lead Lucia to God. In fact, Our Lady held a dialogue with Lucia, the eldest, while the two younger ones watched speechless: Jacinta heard but Francisco only saw. So he, always quick in desiring to understand, asked Lucia:

> *"Why did Our Lady have a Heart in her hand, spreading out over the world that great light which is God? You were with Our Lady in the light which went down towards the earth, and Jacinta was with me in the light which rose towards heaven!"*

This dual direction of the light is very important. As Lucia would explain to Francisco, the two younger ones would soon go to Heaven, so the light was already projecting in that direction, while Lucia would still remain on earth.

Consoling offended Jesus

Francisco loved to pray in secret, alone. He wanted to remain *alone with the Lord* and console Jesus. His joy lay in the fact that soon he would see the Lord. Often he moved away from the other two little shepherd children, hid behind a hedge or a wall so as not to be seen and remain praying. He wanted to pray alone because thus he was able to think better about the Lord and console Him, because He "*is so sad*", he repeated. One day Lucia asked him:

> "*Francisco, which do you like better – to console Our Lord, or to convert sinners, so that no more souls will go to Hell?*" "*I would rather console Our Lord. Didn't you notice how sad Our Lady was that last month, when she said that people must not offend Our Lord any more, for He is already much offended? I would like to console Our Lord, and after that, convert sinners so that they won't offend Him anymore*".

We can say that consoling the Hearts of Jesus and Mary, because they are so offended by the sins of humanity, was the main mission of Saint Francisco of Fatima. While Saint Jacinta was taken by the thought of converting sinners, praying for the Holy Father and freeing souls from Hell, Francisco made his short existence an offering to bring joy to the Lord and so alleviate the pains of His Heart united to the Heart of His Mother. Francisco wanted to remain as long as he could with Jesus in order to console Him. Typical of a child who more than an adult has a profound sense of the pain of abandonment, the disregard of others, or perhaps his parents' lack of affection, our little shepherd made his own the sentiments of the Heart of Christ: he became so intimate with the Lord that he desired solely *to be with Him*, to keep Him company, to give Him all his affection. If sin is an offence against the Lord, contempt for Christ and the choice of another good in place of God, Francisco, on the contrary, by his *staying with Jesus*, wanted to make reparation for this disdain and thus comfort the Heart of his beloved.

Finally, he loved with a totally unique love the Most Holy Sacrament which he defined in a simple but so beautiful way as "hidden Jesus". He often and most willingly remained with Jesus present in the Tabernacle. Sometimes he confided in Lucia:

> *"Listen! You go to school, and I'll stay here in the church, close to the Hidden Jesus. It's not worth my while learning to read, as I'll be going to heaven very soon. On your way home, come here and call me".*

Or:

> *"Look! Go to the church and give my love to the Hidden Jesus. What hurts me most is that I cannot go there myself and stay a while with the Hidden Jesus".*

When he received Holy Communion for the last time before dying he was radiant with joy because, he said, *"I have the Hidden Jesus within my heart"*. Heaven was drawing close. This pure soul was ready to fly there and finally spend all his time with Jesus, now no longer hidden but revealed to his face. Francisco wanted to confess all his sins before dying. But he wanted to be certain of really confessing all of them, without forgetting any. So he asked first Lucia and then Jacinta if they had noticed any sin. Speaking to Lucia, the angelic little shepherd, ready to take off like a little bird on the last flight, said:

> *"I am going to confession so that I can receive Holy Communion, and then die. I want you to tell me if you have seen me commit any sin, and then go and ask Jacinta if she has seen me commit any". "You disobeyed your mother a few times", Lucia said to him, "when she told you to stay at home, and you ran off to be with me or to go and hide". "That's true. I remember that. Now go and ask Jacinta if she remembers anything else".*

Lucia went to Jacinta who, after some thought, replied:

"Well, tell him that, before Our Lady appeared to us, he stole a coin from our father to buy a music box from José Marto of Casa Velha! and when the boys from Aljustrel threw stones at those from Boleiros, he threw some too!"

When Lucia gave him his sister's reply, he said:

"I've already confessed those, but I'll do so again. Maybe, it is because of these sins that I committed that Our Lord is so sad! But even if I don't die, I'll never commit them again. I'm heartily sorry for them now".

And, joining his hands, he repeated the prayer which Our Lady had taught him:

"O my Jesus, forgive us, save us from the fire of hell, lead all souls to heaven, especially those who are most in need".

He received Holy Communion and flew to Heaven. It was 4 April 1919. His little sister Jacinta died the following year, in Lisbon hospital.

The co-redemptive mystery

The heroic life of Saint Francisco Marto, and particularly the emphasis which he places on the mystery of the consolation of the offended Jesus, makes us reflect on the importance of co-redemption, that is, the active participation in the mystery of the Redemption for the salvation of humanity. In Saint Francisco of Fatima this mystery appears more as a desire to save sinners, as a desire to make reparation with love and closeness for the offences against the Hearts of Jesus and Mary. Reparation through the offering of sacrifices thus goes directly to the heart: love for Jesus and Mary. Only thus are sinners released from the snares of their sins and can open themselves to the salvation of Christ. The love which makes a person one with Christ, which takes upon itself the pains of the Beloved, introduces into the heart of the Church an influx of grace so abundant that souls are quickly flooded by it.

We were saying that in Jacinta love for sinners stood out more, while in Francisco it was the desire for solitude to keep the offended Jesus company. These two loves are of course convergent. Both are co-redemptive and at the same time one informs the other: the consolation of the abandoned and offended Jesus saves sinners and love for sinners, the sacrificial offering on their behalf consoles Jesus and drives Him irresistibly to recall them to conversion. Francisco and Jacinta in their young but so profound spirituality complement each other and urge us to do likewise. Two innocent children have made their own internal love of Jesus for souls and the pain of Jesus in seeing Himself rejected and disdained by those who are indifferent. Are we not capable of doing the same?

Francisco, especially, led by the charism of contemplation, ventured out along this path of the love which heals, which loves and consoles. Jesus seemed sad in his contemplation.

Let us return in a more systematic manner to this issue. Sin in fact truly offends the Lord and the Heart of His Mother. Each sin is a nail driven into the Heart of Jesus and Mary. A thorn which wounds and which causes bleeding. All the pain of these wounds caused by each individual sin have been borne by Jesus in His body and by Mary in Her soul and have been nailed once for all to the hard wood of the Cross. Francisco, and the little shepherd children in general, make reference to the offended Jesus a number of times, to God who is so offended by our sins, to the sad Jesus. They are expressions which depict with very intense shades the pain of Jesus in his agonising Passion. The pain, the offence, the sadness which filled the chalice of the Lord. Jesus truly suffered. His pain is not illusory because Jesus was true man. Therefore that chalice Jesus drank from *once for all* in the torment of His Passion and Death. Therefore the risen and glorified Jesus no longer suffers. In Heaven there is no room for sadness and suffering: they have been vanquished forever by Love. Therefore when the little shepherd children, and especially Francisco, make reference to sad Jesus, to Jesus alone, they are experiencing in the space of their lives the agonising Passion and Death of Jesus and the Compassion of Mary. These two august mysteries are incarnated, so to speak, in their vital time and space. The pain of the Cross is imprinted in the *forever* of the redemptive Love. Whoever unites themselves to this pain lives it in their time, but the pain, the insults and death as such, remain in *their* time; by virtue of the glorified and risen Lord, beyond time, they are salvific forever. Our contemplation, our co-redemptive pain, like that of Francisco and Jacinta, open wide, in every time, their salvific efficacy on behalf of our brothers and sisters to be saved. Thus we become co-redeemers on behalf of humanity, but not without entering first of all – like Francisco – into the pulse of love for the Heart of Christ and of Mary.

Why don't we do the same? We enter with love and compassion into the pulse of love for the Hearts of Jesus and of Mary: we will see with the eyes of charity Jesus derided, forgotten, sad and we will console Him. We will see the divine Mother who dries with Her clothes, with Her love, the Blood which pours forth from the Lord's Body so that no one insults Him anymore. In the end, to be a Christian means to become co-redeemers.

THE IMMACULATE HEART, SUMMARY OF THE MESSAGE OF FATIMA

Now the little shepherd children lead us gently to the centre of the heavenly Message. We believe that the whole of the Message of Fatima can be well summarised in the gift of the Immaculate Heart of Mary. The heart is the centre of the person, the Immaculate Heart is the centre of the Message of Fatima: this great gift which God gives us is a gift of salvation.

To understand, however, why Our Lady speaks about the Immaculate Heart at Fatima, it is useful to recall the moments when She spoke of Her Immaculate Heart. It is present first of all in the Angel's apparition, when the heavenly Messenger teaches the second reparatory prayer which towards the end, after the entreaty of reparation towards the Most Holy Eucharist, goes as follows:

> "And through the infinite merits of His most Sacred Hart, and the Immaculate Heart of Mary, I beg of You the conversion of poor sinners".

Here the Heart of Mary, alongside that of Jesus, is presented as the source of merits, of His co-redemptive merits. It is spoken about in the June 1917 apparition. Our Lady tells Lucia about the providential will of God for our time: "He [God] wants to establish in the world devotion to my Immaculate Heart". From the merits of this Heart we come to the need that it be known and loved. "Devotion" will be clarified in the perspective of *consecration*, that is, *refuge* in Mary. Our Lady promises Francisco and Jacinta that soon they will be brought to Heaven, while She says to Lucia:

> "You are to stay here some time longer. Jesus wishes to make use of you to make me known and loved. He wants to establish in the world devotion to my Immaculate Heart", and adds: "Don't lose heart. I will never forsake you. My Immaculate Heart will be your refuge and the way that will lead you to God".

The Immaculate Heart is mentioned again in the second part of the Secret – which contains the true and proper "Secret of Fatima" – after the vision of Hell. The antinomy of Hell is precisely the Immaculate Heart. Our Lady says:

"You have seen Hell where the souls of poor sinners go. To save them, God wishes to establish in the world devotion to my Immaculate Heart".

The Heart of Mary is the alternative to destruction, to ruin. One of the reparatory goals of little Jacinta and Francisco, as we were saying, was that of making reparation for sins committed against the Immaculate Heart of Mary pierced by thorns. The Virgin continues:

"I shall come to ask for the consecration of Russia to my Immaculate Heart, and the Communion of reparation on the First Saturdays".

Finally, again in the same apparition, the mention of the triumph of this Heart: *"In the end, my Immaculate Heart will triumph"*. As can be seen, the Immaculate Heart of Mary is a very frequent theme in the Message: it is a thread which links the different themes and provides their hermeneutical key. But to understand more precisely why it constitutes the synthesis of Fatima, it will be necessary to examine the doctrine which lies at the basis of the term "heart" in biblical teaching, so as then to enter properly into the merits of the Immaculate Heart of Mary as revealed from Heaven at Fatima.

"Heart" in Sacred Scripture

Let us recall first of all the notion of "heart" according to Sacred Scripture. Why the "heart"? Such a concept, which recurs often in the Bible, does not indicate just the organ of the human body, but is often a symbol which indicates the whole person, the seat of thoughts, affections, sentiments, the choices of men and women. For Sacred Scripture, the human person lives in their heart.

In the great prophecies of the Old Testament, in Isaiah, Jeremiah, and above all in Ezekiel, we read:

"A new heart I will give you, and a new spirit I will put within you; and I will remove from your body the heart of stone and give you a heart of flesh" (*Ezek* 36:26).

When the prophets speak to the Israelites to exhort them to leave sin and renew their lives, converting to God and renouncing the idols which entails prostitution – in the language of the Prophets that means betraying the one true God by turning to non-existent gods – they speak of a "renewal of the heart", of a "conversion of heart", because the "heart" for the Bible is the vital centre of the human person.

The *Psalms* speak of the *"meditation of the heart"* (*Ps* 19:14). For Sacred Scripture the heart thinks, in the sense that thoughts reside in the heart, just as in the heart there are sentiments, and the actions of men and women have always been generated from the heart. In fact, this is the teaching of Jesus in the Gospel: *"It is not what goes into the mouth that defiles a person, but it is what comes out of the mouth that defiles"* (*Matt* 15:11), because what comes out of the person comes from their vital centre, which is the heart. Jesus, teaching that the morality of the Christian life does not depend on the purity of the food which is eaten, abolishes the tradition dear to Judaism – and subsequently to Islam, too – of discarding certain foods because they are considered impure. For the Christian, impurity is not caused by foods which, as God's creation, are pure. What makes men and women impure are instead evil actions, contrary to God, which start out from the heart. From it come evil thoughts, fornication, adultery, murder, impurity, and so on, as Saint Paul would say (cf. *1 Cor* 6:7).

The Gospel, too, refers to the heart as the vital centre of the human person. That is the only way the beatitude about which Jesus speaks can be understood: *"Blessed are the pure in heart, for they will see God"* (*Matt* 5:8). Who sees God? Those who have a pure heart, free from the sins which offend God; those who have a heart completely focussed on Him.

Blessed, therefore, are those who live with a pure heart, who live a pure life.

At the same time, this heart becomes a way of union between people and God: it becomes the point of contact. Sacred Scripture does not distinguish between soul and body with a precise philosophical language. Nor does it distinguish between conscience, intelligence, memory, but limits itself to summarising everything by saying: "The pure person knows God". The impure person is far from God, does not succeed in seeing God, has a dirty heart and so is not capable of God; his or her actions, which issue from filth, distance them evermore from God.

Sacred Scripture, which always points out what is essential, cautions against the risk of an impure heart. In the concept of impurity is summed up all the injustice which a heart can harbour against God. There is a serious risk that in life one forgets God: that is what Our Lady showed at Fatima. It is a real, effective danger: that of remaining so imbued with evil as to not outline any other choice but eternal perdition, Hell; when, sadly, this "impure" sin of a heart which no longer sees God is not absolved, therefore restored and redeemed, it remains and is a snare which drags the heart down, and so the human person, to perdition. Men and women become almost impotent because their hearts are incapable of God, are no longer pure, no longer open to truth, to justice, to love. The impure heart does not love truth and justice.

But the Lord does not limit Himself to warning about such a risk, but also shows the alternative to the impurity which leads to trampling on holiness: the true model of a new, pure heart, belonging to God and always open to Him, is the Immaculate Heart of Mary. Mary is She who *"treasured all these things and pondered them in her heart"* (*Lk* 2:19). Mary *treasures* the things of God, the words of the Son and this makes Her Heart pure, the dwelling-place of God.

Two terms are very important: "Heart" and "Immaculate". The attribution *"immaculate"* of the Heart of Mary is fundamental: it presents us, in opposition to the danger of a heart corrupted by sin, with a heart which has never experienced corruption, which knows neither impurity nor sin, does not know opposition to God, rejection of Him, pride, arrogance, the desire to put oneself in His place. It is an incorruptible heart, just as if it had come from divine hands, a most beautiful, most pure Heart, which always sings the glory of God. And it is the Heart of a lady, the Immaculate Heart of Mary.

In the light of what has been set out, to speak now of the "Immaculate Heart" means summarising the "being" of Mary; the "Heart" summarises the person of Mary; the soul, the body, Her conscience, Her thoughts, Her sentiments, Her attitudes. Mary lives in Her Heart and for a time Her Immaculate Heart is the place where God lives. Mary lives in Herself where God lives, in Her Heart.

The immaculateness of the Heart of Mary

Let us reflect again briefly on this quality: the immaculateness of the Heart of Mary. The term "immaculate" expresses the absence of sin – from the slightest stain of sin, even original sin – and, at the same time, the fullness of the grace of Christ.

So two dimensions of "immaculateness", one negative and one positive, can be noticed. The negative dimension indicates the "absence of sin"; the positive is instead the "fullness of the grace of Christ", through a most singular privilege by which God desired to enrich this Lady, so that She might become His worthy Mother. God created humanity, the world, but reserved for Himself a creation more beautiful than the whole of humanity; more beautiful because She was never contaminated by sin, truly free. Freedom is a great gift which God has given us so that we might recognise Him as our Father and go to Him. Mary is the pure prototype of true freedom; She is a free creation, but always directed to God, never in the slightest touched by sin.

So in the Immaculate Heart of Mary it is possible to contemplate what God had originally created for each person, what each person must once again reach as their end: a heart always directed towards God, an immaculate heart.

God's heaven and earth are in this Heart. That most pure creation shaped by God's hands, never "soiled" by the arrogant presence, the pride of humanity, which believes itself to be God and wants to take God's place, is precisely this Immaculate Heart, this new person, the "new Eve", Our Lady.

In a certain sense, to say "*Immaculate Heart*" is the same as saying "*God's heart*", because it is a heart always directed to God. This Heart always says "yes" to God and so overcomes the pride of humanity, the arrogance; it crushes the head of the proud serpent and all the proud children of that serpent. The Immaculate Heart of Mary is a most humble Heart, it is the Heart of She who is the humble "*Handmaid of the Lord*" (*Lk* 1:38. For this reason Our Lady is always free and always of God, who abides in Her Immaculate Heart. The Immaculate Heart is the annihilation of the devil and the arrogant impurity of men and women.

Remedy also for modern pride

In every sin there resides that devilish pride which tries to introduce disobedience to God, indifference to His will, through the same malicious tactic used in the garden of Eden, suggesting to "eat the forbidden fruit", so that we will ourselves become judges of good and evil. The devil deceives the human person who would become God, but against Him and without Him. Often we want to assume this task: being the creators of good and evil, judges of the world, the unique protagonists of our own lives, a life without God in which evil is carried out, which therefore becomes necessary, almost a good. This is the most terrible and most devilish pitfall: to convince oneself that sin is good for us and one cannot live without sinning. It becomes a necessity and even a "grace" – when the young are encouraged to sin first and then to discern whether or not to choose the celibate life in Priesthood – because "it really makes them men". This is the devilish temptation: to become men by sinning – "to get to know the world" is the *polite* version – by disobeying God's Law.

What happened instead to Adam and Eve when first they were captivated by the infernal lie? The Sacred Text states: "*They knew that they were naked*" (*Gen* 3:7), that is they lost what they had received as gift, those gifts of grace which made them creatures already worthy of Heaven.

The devil with his seductions convinces men and women they are really capable of being themselves, of knowing how to impose themselves when choosing evil. In every sin is hidden that presumption of wanting to experience, to understand, to know. The original seduction is represented in every sin. Only after having committed it does one experience one's real misery; it is not true that we have become like God, in fact we have become lesser human beings, losing something of our own dignity, losing that most beautiful gift which instead really made us great, divine grace, friendship with God, the possibility of seeing God, knowing His will and fulfilling it.

Lucifer and sin, however, are not satisfied: after defeat they still fight stubbornly against God, because they want to usurp being God and believe that by a life parallel to God, a life of misery and sin, can the Lord be defeated, to the point of usurping His throne. Hell is the consequence of the presumption of wanting to reign in His place. It is the pride which remains, the arrogance which says: I am god!

Instead in the Immaculate Heart of Mary we find refuge and salvation. To consecrate oneself to the Immaculate Heart means fleeing from this seduction to become God without God, which the world continually presents. "Your eyes will be opened and you will become like God!" (cf. *Gen* 3:5): this was the deceit!

Instead, how does one really become like God? When we participate in grace in the life of God. Jesus says to His disciples: "Very truly, I tell you, the one who believes in me will also do the works that I do and, in fact, will do greater works than these..." (cf. *Jn* 14:12). We can become God only through *participation* in the gift of sanctifying grace. It is important to have a humble heart through which we have the never-ending vision of God, by which we are not convinced of being God, but with love we carry out His will in obtaining salvation.

The centre of the Immaculate Heart is seeing God. Mary sees God since Her Heart is that centre of love in which there echoes ceaselessly the *Fiat* to God's will. Mary gives Her *Fiat* so that Heaven is united to earth, God becomes man and lives in our midst.

Our Lady has been given to us as a gift as the "Immaculate Heart". She Herself gives us Her Heart which we need so much to defeat pride, arrogance, the impurity of wanting to take God's place, to be above His Commandments. It is a seduction today more pressing than ever, which has made us authors of a new morality to justify the devilish claim for doing evil. But the sole pretext is according to the flesh. A return to paganism. It is a temptation presented on a silver plate: for example, it is said that it is not the number of sins or acts which offend God, but the real offence consists in separating oneself from God by an explicit act of denial; so, according to this theory which is defined as the "fundamental option", as long as there is not a declared intention to reject God as a general act, even if in everyday practical life one commits sinful acts, the sin does not exist, since this general leaning towards God which justifies all sins remains internally. A good excuse to no longer give any significance to individual acts.

Isn't it instead true that in every act we chose evil or good? A drug user who experiences moments of ecstasy would not fool themselves about getting out of that condition of terrible slavery if they thought that all things considered the love of the freedom not to use drugs would be sufficient to defeat the seduction. Every action counts. Every action is good or evil.

There is only one Truth

We return to those words of Saint Paul: "*For you were called to freedom, brothers and sisters; only do not use your freedom as an opportunity for self-indulgence*" (*Gal* 5:13). The carnal human being is no longer capable of God, is no longer aware that it is concrete actions and not general intentions, the daily choices, which shape life and make men and women great if they are choices made with God, but make them wretched if they are contrary to God's Commandments. This is well known, because it is there for all to see! Men and women are what they love and become what they want. The great mystery is the freedom which drives to choose and act. It is not true that a generic leaning towards God is sufficient to be saved; it would be like cancelling people's lives, saying that life consists in one choice and that would not make right all the anguish, the hope, the choices, everything which constitutes our lives. It is instead a deceit, which leads to living without God, self-justification.

The original temptation, unfortunately, is presented in our days with renewed false theories which drive people to commit sin with the pretext that this makes us great, with no more fear of God. One even reaches the absurd statement that good and evil co-exist in God: everything resides in God and therefore there is no longer any difference between a good and an evil act. This apparent distinction would be precisely mere appearance for the as yet unenlightened poor mortals, but without any significance, because, in fact, good and evil would be two sides of the same coin. It is easy to understand how a vision of this kind tends to justify the greatest atrocities, like, for example, abortion and euthanasia. It would mean saying that to kill a child or give it life is the same thing; that to kill a sick person in a terminal state or to encourage him or her to respect their life and to do the will of God are the same. Good and evil, life and death become the same thing: mere appearance.

Today's seduction is clothed in new categories, which appear more philosophical, more intelligent, more scientific, but are no more than a disguise of the ancient error which leads people far from God.

What is the solution so as not to fall into the trap of this new and terrible seduction? It is necessary that Our Lady intervenes with the gift of Her Immaculate Heart as "refuge" from these subtle and flattering temptations. To say nothing then about evolutionism, now a ruling dogma in culture.

Today, many people think that everything is a casual product of an eternal evolution and to state that God has created things from nothing is almost blasphemy, because it would put in a difficult position the theory according to which human beings and the things which exist derive from inferior species. That is, there is a desire to state that things were not created by God, but come from an autonomous development of matter which is always evolving. The problem, however, is that very few reflect on the fact that an eternal matter fruit of itself and cause of itself and of all other things is simply absurd. Either matter is God or created by God. Since God is not matter, that is, God is not material, the only alternative can be that everything which exists is created by God, that matter is created by God.

However, in following this evolutionistic thought, clearly, many lose the true way, no longer see God. It is clear: if life is the fruit of casual evolution, what is the point of doing God's will? Who is God if at the origins of life there is chance? Why convert? Convert from what? Unfortunately this idea is dear to so many Catholics, too. When they hear talk about creation and that God is the Creator of all that exists, they are scandalised! They are fables which can be told to children, but they cannot be told to adults.

This problem, applied then in the ambit of Faith, reduces the work of Jesus Christ, His supernatural Redemption, no longer to a sacrificial offering by Jesus who pays for us, to ransom us from sin and reconcile us with God, but to a work of love, of sharing by a good man who came to speak of peace, universal brotherhood, stimulating us to be friends with nature, to respect the environment, to be ecologists, even to be brothers and sisters to the animals and plants. These are not fantasies, but arguments which attempt to prove and inoculate through aberrant mass-media campaigns. Thus is presented a Jesus debased in his essence: no longer a God-man who became flesh for our salvation, but a superior man, better than others, who teaches to be better with everyone.

With a vision of this kind, where the supernatural aspect of Faith is missing, gradually all the truths of Faith are called into question, with belief in a Jesus who is a fruit of fantasy or convenience and not in the Jesus who became flesh and which the Church's *Credo* makes us profess as Son of God who suffered, died and rose for us.

In the end, for so many Christians today this vision is winning, because it marries well with the other religions or with those who do not believe in God. With the pretext of having finally to avoid disputes offending those who do not believe in God – dodging any reference to evil, to sin, to conversion – it is said that it is better to adopt a more ecological, more practical Christian theory which harmonises more easily with all the other ways of thinking; with the aim of discovering that Jesus who makes Himself a brother to everyone, capable of uniting everyone together, at least in respect for creation. The ecological theory seems to have a strong bite in ecumenism, too.

When John Paul II died, a nun was interviewed, and asked what thing of beauty had that pontificate left her. Perhaps ingenuously, she replied as follows: "This Pope was great especially because he taught us that all religions are equal". In truth, this was not the teaching of the Pope, but due to so many of the gestures of that Pope, it is the perception that many have, including priests and religious.

We have fallen ill to the disease of relativist syncretism, a most grave sin which reduces Christ and the Gospel to a fantastic projection. "Relativism" means that truth does not exist, no absolute truth, that all truths are equal, since no one can pretend to state a reality with certainty. The truth does not exist, so no one can impose it; even less can Catholics dare to say that Christ is the Truth. Consequently, Catholics should find a path to adapt to such general relativism and they will find it in that of a Jesus more man than God, more human, more ecological.

Do we understand that of necessity we need a refuge, to find a pure place in the Church where we can preserve faith and hope? Where we are not dragged into the mud of doctrinal and moral impurity? Here once again is the remedy for these seductions: the Immaculate Heart of Mary. It warns us against this ruling vision. What a grace to be consecrated to the Immaculate Heart of Mary! It is the grace not to fall into these traps which are like a tasty but poisoned food; they offer the possibility of us all seeing ourselves as brothers and sisters, of all being together, but without the need to reject idols, to deny the false claims, the errors, to convert to God, the one Truth, to eliminate our arrogance and our comforts. The grace of being consecrated to the Immaculate Heart of Mary ensures that these problems are understood and we become true apostles of Jesus.

To be consecrated to the Heart of Mary, the "refuge" which Our Lady gives us at Fatima, means to make one's own Our

Lady's "yes" to God, leaning always towards Him, to see Him and say "yes" to His will. To find the Heart of Mary is then to find the true Church, the place of purity of faith and morals. The place of God.

Humanity at a crossroads

So, there is a need to enter this Ark of salvation. It was in the ark that Noah found salvation from the flood, so the children of Mary, who consecrate themselves and welcome Her Immaculate Heart, enter into this fortress, into the Ark of the new Covenant, which contains within itself the things most holy, the mysteries of Faith, the things and mysteries of God, contains the true Jesus – not the one "made" by men and women, nothing but a special man – the God who made Himself man. This Ark is the womb which contains Jesus and, therefore, contains all the mysteries of the true Faith which He taught us and which the Church jealously guards.

In concrete terms, the Immaculate manifests the deceit of the modern world to those who show themselves to be Her faithful children, in such a way that they realise that that fruit, even if beautiful to see, is not something good but a poisonous fruit; even if that way of thinking is common to the majority of people, we realise that it is mistaken, because it is not in conformity with the doctrine of the Church, with the Catechism of the Church. So, when we hear it said, for example, that Communion can be received even if someone is in a state of mortal sin, reserving confession until they have more time; or, as many people say, that it is sufficient to "confess to the Lord", so one can sin and then resolve everything by turning to Him directly, then the true child of the Immaculate Heart of Mary will recognise the subtle deceit, not at all new, which leads to living in a way contrary to God's Law and which leads to perdition. To unite oneself with such a worldly thought, to persist in this way of life, roots the human person so much in evil as to give them a habit which distances them evermore from God and makes us always more accustomed to our ideas, to our *I*. On the contrary, the Heart of Mary Most Holy is a Heart which simply says '*Fiat voluntas tua*': "*I am the handmaid of the Lord*" (*Lk* 1:38).

Pope John Paul II consecrated the world to the Immaculate Heart of Mary in 1984; when he repeated this act in the Jubilee of 2000, he said that "today, more than ever in the past, humanity is at a crossroads": general destruction or salvation. And, strangely enough, today general destruction is much easier than it once was, all that is needed is the press of a button. Think of the nuclear bomb: very quickly, the whole of humanity, or a great part of it, would disappear! Is the flaming sword in the hands of the Angel about to strike against humanity more impending than it was 40 or 50 years ago?

With really significant and sometimes important and useful progress, such as technological, not just good but evil, too, has increased, because sight of the measure of goodness, the moral rule which must guide us in development, has been lost. Destruction is at the door.

Who can be saved from the danger of this destruction, which of course is not just the nuclear bomb? The greatest ruin is false hope, not in God and in His just remuneration, but in ourselves, in our technological progress. The most harmful risk today is to encounter destruction without realising it: self-destruction pursued in the belief that one is doing oneself good. There is that pride in believing oneself to be so advanced because, not only have we succeeded in landing on the Moon, we have even found the way to make children in-vitro by manipulating people's lives, the thing most sacred! We have become so intelligent as to reproduce people in series, like machines do, because in the end – this is the modern thought – people are just machines but a bit more developed.

Instead no one can put their hands on life and on the most sacred things of humanity! This is self-destruction! That is not the progress of humanity, but another form of that eugenics for which Hitler was reproached and which today instead is much more camouflaged, carried out in laboratories: in fact not all the children produced in series will be able to live, but only those strong ones who resist. So many children produced are simply destined to feed the process of mechanical reproduction, but we know they will not succeed in living. They are frozen and then destroyed.

The Immaculate Heart of Mary preserves us from such moral corruption. Humanity is at a crossroads. Where is salvation? How can one realise there is a need to be saved? If humanity continues along this path, if it continues to reason in this way, it is heading towards its destruction.

The alternative to decay exists: it is the Immaculate Heart of Mary. We who are members of the Church can repair the crumbling walls of this Church if we welcome the Immaculate Heart of Mary. She asks this of each of us: to renounce sin, to renounce a life without God and to live as children of Her Immaculate Heart.

This is the mystery of Fatima, the great opportunity which God offers to defeat pride, the arrogance of evil which is destruction. The alternative, the hope, the salvation is the Virgin Mary, that pure Heart where God resides, that Heart which sees God; consequently, whoever consecrates themselves to this Heart is capable of seeing God, because the Immaculate clothes everyone consecrated to Her in Her purity, Her humility, Her obedience to God and to God's Commandments.

Part Three

The Message of Fatima
in the light of the Gospel

At Fatima like the Disciples of Emmaus

Overall, the Message of Fatima in a certain sense admonishes us with the same words of Our Lord reported by the holy Gospel in the meeting of the Risen One with the two disciples of Emmaus (cf. *Lk* 24:13-53. It must be recognised how often hearts are closed and minds slow to understand the words of the prophets, in understanding the Scriptures and believing that Jesus has truly risen.

As with the disciples of Emmaus, so it is in daily life, in family, social, working life, where it is easy to lose sight of the Lord, He is forgotten and it often happens that with the passage of time people become increasingly incredulous. Believing becomes a burden. The misfortunes of life and the vicissitudes of our time give rise to very pessimistic and egocentric reflections. In the end, one wonders what is the point of believing. Why believe today? What does Faith give us? In a strongly subjective and utilitarian world, where everything is measured on the basis of what can provide an immediate advantage, Faith is useless. What is the point of God? In daily life one becomes increasingly hard of heart in believing in the Word of the Lord, in recognising this truth, therefore in adhering to it with the whole of one's life.

Our Lady appeared at Fatima, in this blessed land, so that our hearts, weighed down by daily exertions and distractions, might be revived by the maternal call, the call of the Blessed Virgin Mary, who presented a prophecy, in other words a word which comes from God and which is inscribed in the unique Word of God, in the unique Word of Truth. Fatima is precisely a prophecy, a heavenly message of salvation, which spurs us to believe in the unique message of salvation, the Gospel: outside the Gospel there is no other truth. Since we can easily doze off forgetting the Gospel, Our Lady Herself came to wake us up and remind us of it. The heart of our Faith is the Resurrection of Jesus: Jesus who destroys death, the power of the devil, of the infernal gods, the iniquitous power of sin and rises, is alive and is the centre of our Faith.

So why do we believe? It is essential to respond to this question: we believe because Jesus, the Son of God, became man to free us from the greatest snare, that of sin. He triumphed over sin, redeemed us, reconciled us with God to open for us the doors of eternal salvation. We believe because Jesus is not an invention, but a fact; His Resurrection is a fact: since that tomb is empty and Jesus is alive and appeared to the disciples, we welcome His Word of truth, the Word of the Prophets, of the Scriptures, which Jesus explains to the disciples of Emmaus.

What did Our Lady do at Fatima? In a certain sense She followed the same pedagogical itinerary of the Lord on the road to Emmaus, so that we might believe in the one Truth: that Jesus suffered for our sins and died for us. Christ has freed us from eternal death. Wasn't it necessary for the Master to undergo that atrocious torment of His Passion to save us and thus enter into His glory? Of course. And didn't Our Lady tell us – through the preparation of Her Message – that the one way to salvation is renunciation, penance and conversion?

Comparing the Message of Fatima and the holy Gospels, one notes a unique affinity. Let us briefly recall an aspect of it to see how Fatima recalls the Gospel in its essential lines, in its fundamental features, in fact it could be said that Fatima is nothing but the Gospel explained today to an atheistic and materialistic world, marked by a "world war in segments". We know well that it can never be said that the snare of war has ceased, since wars follow one another continually; to say nothing of that most frightening thing, which could signal the disappearance of the whole of humanity in the blink of an eye: nuclear war.

In this increasingly inhuman world, Our Lady comes to state the one truth: to save us it is essential to die to sin, to offer ourselves in sacrifice to God, so that we can rise with Jesus and therefore ascend to Heaven. To enter Heaven we must necessarily imitate Jesus, welcome His Word; only in this way can we die definitively to that most terrible snare, which is sin and thus be saved.

The reality of salvation as liberation from sin, and therefore as rebirth in Christ, is prepared by Mary Most Holy through the apparitions of the Angel. We have seen how the apparitions of Our Lady from May to October were prepared by the Angel of God. Three times the Angel appeared and taught the little shepherd children a prayer of reparation for all the tremendous sins committed against the Most Holy Trinity: sins against faith; sins against hope; sins against charity: *"My God, I believe, I adore, I hope and I love You!...".*

The prayers of the Angel

In the world into which the Angel came down in that period of 1915-1916 there had been a terrible revolution, the Communist Revolution, which had marked the start of a State atheism, an atheism imposed with strength as law. Those who instead said "My God, I do not believe, I do not adore, I do not hope in and I do not love you! My God, I reject you!" were able to continue to live peacefully.

The Angel prepared the little shepherd children, in their simplicity, to pray and to make reparation for those tremendous sins which cried out for vengeance in the sight of God, because not to believe, not to adore, not to hope in and not to love God means to start to believe in matter, in the political institutions, in men and women; it means idolising things, putting people in God's place. What did that mean for all of us in the century that we have just left behind? The destruction of humanity, because, if an ideology takes the place of God, if men and women are adored in God's place, men and women – every individual – will pretend to be a master: the strongest person will want to enslave the weakest; there will no longer be mercy or justice, there will no longer be peace. The world becomes a hell. *"My God, I believe, I adore, I hope and I love You!..."*. The Angel taught to pray and to make reparation for this most serious sin, the sin of idolatry, the sin of atheism; not even an atheism in which one is free to reject God, but an imposed atheism, which marked the persecution and destruction of so many of our Christian brothers and sisters. The Angel then taught the little shepherd children another very important prayer in reparation for another very serious sin, that against the Most Holy Eucharist. Adoration of the Most Holy Eucharist is necessary, as is reparation for the sacrilegious sins against it. In fact, the Angel taught the children to *adore* and *o er* reparation for all the sacrileges, for all the omissions and the outrages committed towards this Sacrament. The Eucharist is not the prize of the just, nor even the food of the poor: it is the Body and Blood of the Lord!

One can understand how adoration of the Eucharist can only flow from true faith, hope and charity. The heart of the Church is the Eucharistic Jesus; when Christians live forgetful of it, when they do not conform their lives to it, they commit a most grave sacrilege. When people approach the Eucharist in a state of mortal sin, without recognising that that Bread is the Body of God which has been given to us, when it is profaned, the Faith of the Church is weakened: the sin of one person is certainly harmful to the communion of the mystical Body.

From a lack of faith in God, undoubtable truth, derives necessarily a lack of faith in the mysteries of God, so in the Most Holy Eucharist. So many people easily forget the real mystery of the Eucharist and think that, in the end, it is simply a convivial meal, where everyone participates as if at a beautiful dinner. Everyone goes to it, even those in a state of sin; often, then, people go to receive that Most Holy Bread distracted or taking it in their hands, as if this

Bread were any type of food, a food for a celebration, forgetting the truth of the Eucharist. Saint Peter reminds us:

> *"You know that you were ransomed from the futile ways inherited from your ancestors, not with perishable things like silver or gold, but with the precious blood of Christ, like that of a lamb without defect or blemish"* (*1 Pt* 1:18-19).

The Eucharist is Jesus the Lamb sacrificed and glorified. The apparitions of the Angel prepare those of Our Lady and instil in the hearts of the little shepherd children the knowledge that it is necessary to always start from this supersubstantial Bread. It is necessary to start from reparation for the most serious sin which is committed against the Eucharist, when people forget that it is the Sacrifice of Jesus, it is His Body *given* and His Blood *poured out*. Only by understanding the intimate significance of the Sacrifice of Jesus for our sins can one also understand the dimension of "banquet" and approach the Eucharist not like any type of bread but as the Lamb of God. When there is a true faith, true adoration, true hope and charity, there is true Eucharist. With the Eucharist our eyes are opened, we see the Lord and we adore Him. With His disciples we say: "Stay with us, Lord, so that the evening does not set on our Faith and on Holy Mother Church". In the Eucharist we recognise the Resurrection of Jesus, which is the start of our transformation into *new creatures*: precisely what the Lady dressed in White would ask the three children of Fatima, when She asked them to offer themselves in sacrifice and thus open Heaven to many; which otherwise would remain closed due to the hardness of hearts.

Against the prevalent snares

We can understand even more the topicality of Fatima for our Faith and Christian life referring us to another trap which is dominant today. It is a trap which again threatens the Holy

Eucharist. It is often presented in a very banal way: "We are all risen" is bandied about everywhere and so there is no longer any need, for example, to kneel during the holy Liturgy. So many times we see benches in churches without kneelers; this is not forgetfulness on the part of the manufacturers, but a very precise desire to present a simpler faith by watering it down, the faith in the Risen One which no longer wants to pass through self-humiliation, self-abasement through sacrifice and death with Christ, death to sin, to rise with Him. Those who do not kneel do not rise because in order to rise one needs to die to self.

Instead, what would the Holy Virgin say to the little Visionaries of Fatima, to avoid us still dwelling on unproductive considerations, like those of the two disciples of Emmaus who were returning that day saddened at the death of Jesus? They had lost hope, because He had not liberated them from the power of the Romans, their oppressors. Sometimes we discuss the Faith and we are more concerned about describing it than showing it through works. We are sad because people do not believe, but we do not have the courage to set ourselves the real questions and ask ourselves why people do not believe. We present an easy, attractive Christianity, but renounce evangelising and preaching conversion, the renunciation of idols and false religions. We want people to be risen before dying. Risen without first the death to sin is like thinking of believing without grace. There is no real joy without denial.

Our Lady states that salvation, therefore eternal resurrection with Christ, always passes through renunciation, through conversion of heart, renewal of men and women in their totality. There is no resurrection without death, just as there is no Resurrection without the Passion of Jesus. Just as the Scriptures speak about this in their entirety, so Our Lady spoke about it at Fatima: Faith, the Eucharist, sacrifice as death to sin to rise and be saved from eternal perdition. The Virgin then taught us the value of prayer, the value of the Sacraments, the value of self-offering: a co-redemptive offering for all our brothers and sisters who forget their supernatural vocation.

Without doubt it is a grace to be able to meditate on these aspects of the Message of Fatima, which are nothing other than the prophecy adapted for our times, which exhorts us to understand and live the Gospel today. Fatima is an invitation to take our Christian vocation seriously.

From "being already risen" derives another trap from which liberation is urgent: that of believing that being Christian means being able to live in a carefree manner, because, in the end, "we've already been saved, Jesus has done everything". Jesus has done everything – in our opinion – even what we do not want to do or even the evil we do. This means that poor Jesus is always responsible for good and evil because, in fact, "He has done everything". We no longer have to do anything, it is sufficient to believe in a spontaneous manner, when you have the desire, when you feel like it.

At Fatima Our Lady – as had already been said in the holy Gospel – tells us that this is not true. Yes, Jesus has done everything because He is the Saviour, but what He has done for us He also asks us to do, so that we can be one with Him. To be saved by the Lord does not mean standing and watching and perhaps blaming Him for not doing all that He could have done: this in fact is the thought when God is blamed for the tragedies which befall us. We must participate in our salvation in Jesus. How? In the most beautiful manner: with Our Lady, through the Immaculate Heart of Mary.

With Pope Saint John Paul II we must all say that the Church in the Third Millennium will have to pass through Fatima, the whole of the Church's Faith will have to pass through this great prophecy which Our Lady wanted to give us and which we hope to understand and put into practice.

THE MYSTERY OF THE HOLY EUCHARIST

Reading the paschal account of the Gospel of *John* (6:22-29), Jesus puts a profound question which concerns us, too. He had just multiplied the loaves, appeasing the hunger of the disciples and a large crowd. That gesture was a miraculous gesture aimed at signifying above all another much deeper reality than material bread: He wanted to allude to the miracle of miracles, to the true Bread which comes from Heaven, a piece of bread which, by virtue of Christ's words, becomes His Body. But those very materialistic people – in which it is easy to see ourselves mirrored – followed Jesus because with Him they ate free! They were able to satisfy their hunger without many sacrifices, such was Jesus' goodness. We remember the Lord's admonishment:

> *"Very truly, I tell you, you are looking for me, not because you saw signs, but because you ate your fill of loaves. Do not work for the food that perishes, but for the food that endures for eternal life, which the Son of Man will give you. For it is on him that God the Father has set his seal" (Jn 6:26-27).*

These words of Jesus make us reflect: what does one have to be really concerned about? Worries, the things of daily life, one's own problems? Do we seek Jesus for merely material interest, because we want to resolve a problem? This, too, could be important, but cannot be our main goal.

So why deepen the mystery of Fatima? Why seek Jesus in the Immaculate Heart of Mary? Because we want to rediscover, completely, the truth of this great mystery which is the Eucharist; so great that the Angel prepared the little shepherd children for the mystery of the Eucharist by giving them communion. Before giving them communion with the Most Holy Body of the Lord, he taught them a prayer of reparation so that the children might impress on their hearts what is the Body of Christ, that Body of Jesus present in all the Tabernacles, present in the mystery of the transubstantiation of the bread into the Body and of the wine into the Blood of Jesus.

Fatima enables us to deepen the truth of the Most Holy Eucharist. What is the Eucharist shown to the little shepherd children? A piece of bread? No, it is the Lord, it is the whole Jesus present in that piece of bread. It is not a memory of Jesus, it is not a symbol of the presence of Jesus, it is not bread which appeases us and satisfies us in a material fashion. This Bread is the Lord, it is the Sacrifice of Jesus and His Presence which makes us become one with Him.

So we must ask ourselves: how do we celebrate this Eucharistic Mystery? How do we participate in the Holy Mass? How and with what sentiments do we approach the Holy Eucharist? Do we know what the Eucharist is? Do we adore Eucharistic Jesus before receiving Him? Are we in God's grace when we approach the Eucharist, that is, without mortal sin on our conscience? Do we not risk acting like those crowds which followed Jesus for other interests, for other ends? We want to find Jesus to understand who Jesus is, to adore Him, to make reparation for the sins committed against the Most Holy Eucharist.

To reach this goal it is necessary to follow in the footsteps of the little shepherd children, especially Saints Jacinta and Francisco: then we will really learn what the Eucharist is. We ask precisely from them to teach us to love Jesus in the Eucharist, to make reparation for all the sins committed against this divine Sacrament; that they may give us some of their love, so pure, so simple, so profound for Jesus in the Eucharist, to the point Francisco frequently exclaimed: "*I'll stay here in church, close to hidden Jesus*". While the other children went to school, Francisco preferred to retire to a church and stay there for hours and hours before the hidden Jesus. When he was asked why, he replied: "*Soon, I will go to Heaven*", Our Lady had revealed to him; he wanted to prepare himself in this way, in adoration of Jesus in the Eucharist. Adoration of Jesus in the Eucharist is the way to Heaven: it unites earth to Heaven, it makes us pass from this earth to God's Heaven.

With the holy little shepherd children it is necessary for us, too, to go to Jesus to love Him, adore Him and so become likewise apostles of the Eucharist to live in our lives of faith this mystery which is Sacrifice, the Presence of Jesus and Communion with Him.

The Sacrifice of the Holy Mass

Fatima leads us to rediscover Holy Mass. We meditate on the reality of Mass as it presents itself to our faith and thus how we are called to live it. Chapter 6 (vv. 30-35 of the holy Gospel of John, which contains Jesus' famous discourse on the "Bread of Life", puts before our eyes the key mystery of the Eucharist, the mystery which is the foundation of our Christian Faith, of the Church, therefore of our identity.

When is the Eucharist *made*, so to speak? The Eucharist – the Body, Blood, Soul, Divinity of Jesus – is *made* in the mystery of the Holy Mass. So it is good to examine in depth what is the Holy Mass so that we can better understand the Holy Eucharist.

In effect, the words which in the New Testament refer to the Holy Eucharist are different and all allude to a mystery of divine compliance: God gives Himself as divine Bread and we offer that "broken" Bread as thanksgiving for His supreme gift: the gift of the Son. In fact, the term "Eucharist" means "thanksgiving" and the most common expression used to define it is *"fractio panis"*, the *"breaking of the bread"*, or more accurately *"to break the bread"*. For example, in the *Acts of the Apostles* (2:42; 20:7, we read that the Apostles were united together in prayers and in the breaking of the bread. The disciples of Emmaus had *"recognised [Jesus] in the breaking of the bread"* (*Lk* 24:35. On that occasion Jesus did not celebrate Holy Mass once again, but simply repeated that gesture which instituted the Holy Sacrifice: the offering of Himself, His Body broken for us in His Passion and Death.

The Holy Mass is the holiest, most sacred action, in which the Body of Christ, our Viaticum, the One who gives us the strength to walk and to evangelise others, is given to us. So the Eucharist is the fruit of the Holy Mass and at the same time designates the celebratory action which is thanksgiving and sacrificial offering. In the Holy Sacrifice of the Mass the Eucharist is given to us.

The Holy Mass, therefore, is the liturgical-sacramental action of the Sacrifice of Calvary and therefore of the offering which Jesus made once and for all by immolating Himself. The Eucharist is the Sacrifice of Jesus on the Cross, which gives content to the Eucharist as Sacrament; in fact, on the night He was betrayed, Our Lord instituted the Sacrament of His Body and His Blood; on the same night when He was handed over to the hands of the authorities to be judged and condemned to death, He handed Himself over to us, He offered Himself, in a bloody way, on the Cross. The Eucharistic banquet, which derives from the sacrifice – there is no communion without oblation – is always approaching Communion with Jesus the immolated and glorious Lamb. That is why the banquet aspect of the Eucharist can never be separated from the sacrificial. The sacrifice is for communion and communion is transformation in the sacrifice of the Lord. Let us look in depth at this harmonious relationship.

Jesus took the bread and said: "*This is my body, which is given for you*" (*Lk* 22:19). Then he took the chalice and said: "*This is the blood of the covenant, which is poured out for many for the forgiveness of sins*" (*Matt* 26:28). The Italian liturgical text of the transubstantiation translates "for all" in a very hasty manner, but in reality the exact expression is "for many" (in Greek "*pollôn*"), as the English Missal does.

The sacrificial content of the Eucharist is obvious: the Body of Jesus is a Body given, offered, just as His Blood is poured out.

When does Jesus offer His Body? When is this Blood poured out? When Jesus was raised and pierced on the Cross. There is the offering of His Body and of His Blood, that is, the bloody sacrifice, the immolation of Himself on the altar of Golgotha.

The Holy Mass has as objective content the Sacrifice of Calvary, without which it would be impossible even to understand the gift of the Eucharist as "Communion". Communion with Jesus, being in communion with Him receiving the Eucharist, is born from His sacrificial offering to the point of the gift of Himself on the Cross. The Eucharist is the offering of Jesus to the Father for our salvation, so that we might be *reconciled* with God. To receive Communion without being reconciled with God, living in sin, is to insult the mystery. Reconciliation, becoming *one* with Christ is the aim of the sacrifice. The end clearly does not exclude the start: the oblative desire of the Lord. John tells us that the Lord *"in finem dilexit eos" [loved them to the end]"* (*Jn* 13:1), right up to *"consummatum est"* (*Jn* 19:30).

Then the Lord added: *"Do this in remembrance of me"* (*Lk* 22:19). "Remembrance" is not simply a recollection, like we recall a past action, but it is an action, a liturgical celebration which actualises now, *hic et nunc*, what Jesus did once and for all on the Cross. He said: *"This is my body which is given for you"* on the Cross; *"This is my blood"* shed for you. And He added the commandment: *"Do this in remembrance of me"*, in other words, repeat this gesture, actualise it, doing what I have done. Each time Holy Mass is celebrated we find ourselves at the foot of the Cross of Jesus, on Calvary, and we relive what Jesus has done, offering Himself to the Father as Lamb of God for our salvation. Jesus did not say to the Apostles: "Have dinner" and "Enjoy your meal in my memory", but: "Do this gesture, break the Bread which is broken for you". The broken Bread is Jesus!

Let us say it again, given the dominant protestantisation: the Eucharist will never be a piece of bread, it can never be a "memory" of Jesus, because it is the Sacrament of His Sacrifice. In the Eucharist there is the glorious Victim, Jesus the victim, who offered Himself for us; immolated, but glorious, risen and living, real, present. In the Eucharist there is all of Jesus.

From Sacrifice, Communion

When Our Lady asked the little shepherd children: "*Are you willing to offer yourselves in sacrifice?*", to what could the little shepherd children refer to understand the reality of "sacrifice"? From where could they draw the strength to live it? From the Holy Mass, from the Eucharist. That is why Francisco suddenly changes attitude. The Angel had prepared the little shepherd children for the reparation of sins committed against the Eucharist, because the Eucharist is the source of every sacrifice, it is the supreme Sacrifice of Jesus.

Whoever wants to live the sacrificial offering of self, to respond to the requests of the Holy Virgin, must always draw strength from the Eucharist, must start from the Holy Mass, live it, and so understand exactly what the Mass is. To understand what the Mass is every Christian should be encouraged to experience the so-called "Tridentine" Holy Mass, in the old and uninterrupted form of the Roman Missal.

Our sacrifice can be accepted by God only when it is offered with Jesus, in Jesus, in the Holy Mass. We are often terrified by the word "sacrifice" because we do not experience the mystery of the Holy Mass. When we experience Mass, when it becomes our life and our life is directed continually towards it, not only do we understand the preciousness of the sacrifice but we seek it as the favourite path to Jesus and to Mary. If we live the Mass we learn to *communicate ourselves*, to drink only at the source of Life: at the pierced side of the Lord.

We have said that the dimension of Communion originates immediately in the sacrificial content of the Eucharist. The

Eucharist is Sacrifice and, consequently, is Communion, in other words it is to become Jesus in receiving Him as food.

We return once again to this so vital and precious aspect so as not to lose faith in the gift of Jesus. From sacrifice come the origins of the Eucharistic banquet and never the other way round; there is no need to invert the properties of the Eucharist by stating that the banquet "reminds us" of the Sacrifice of the Cross! Often Mass is experienced in this manner: everyone gathers around the altar together, it is believed that everyone is equal almost as if there were no difference between priest and the faithful, so *everyone* celebrates Mass and *everyone* receives the Eucharist communicating themselves (one witnesses real Eucharistic mockeries when the faithful go the altar and self-communicate. That standing together, that fraternal banquet, would remind us what Jesus has done for us. That is profoundly mistaken.

The banquet, Communion, is devoid of meaning if it does not stem from the Sacrifice of Jesus. There must be the Sacrifice of the One who *humiliated* Himself for us, who gave Himself to us and so only thus can we, from the bottom, as humble sinners, approach Jesus and be raised on high, into Communion with Him. It is very important to put together these two elements correctly and in hierarchical order so as not to risk manipulating abusively the liturgy, the Mass, and consequently Christian life, too. When it is said, in the end, that everyone celebrates Mass, that the Mass is a fraternal assembly, it is a mere banquet, it is an attempt to contrast the sacrificial dimension with that of the banquet. To think about having a feast is to forget what the Eucharist is about. We celebrate Mass for our feast, but without the Lord with us. We must not clumsily, when not ideologically, extract the notion of "sacrifice" from that of "banquet", but vicev-ersa, that of "feast" from that of "sacrificial oblation". Communion with Jesus is true communion with Him if it is a gift which comes from the Most High: "*I am the living bread that came down from heaven*"

(*Jn* 6:51). Communion is a gift from on High because it is the *esinanitio* of Jesus, His bowing to our miseries. Jesus, while being God, became man, a slave, to the point of dying as a wrongdoer. Only thus can we participate in the Eucharist: if we make our own these sentiments of Jesus, if we approach the Eucharist with sentiments of the servant who belittles, who humiliates himself; the servant who is reborn from on High.

From this there now arises the almost spontaneous question about the most worthy manner in which to receive the Eucharist. If the Holy Mass is the Sacrifice-Sacrament which gives us the Eucharist, then it can be understood without too much difficulty that the most worthy manner to receive it cannot be standing up or in the hand. The Eucharist is the Sacrifice which gives us Life. For this reason the Church, in her uninterrupted Tradition, has understood that the most beautiful and holiest way to receive the Eucharist is on one's knees and in the mouth. And so it was up until a few years ago when it was decided to change the practice. But with what gain? Have our faithful better understood what the Mass is, what is Communion? Mass must also consist in our humiliation before Jesus, so that we are raised by Him for the glory of God.

If our Communion with Him, and in Him with our brothers and sisters, derives from the Sacrifice of Jesus, from the sacrifice we also learn our becoming Eucharist and thanksgiving with Jesus to the Father. Hence the importance of pausing, having received Holy Communion, in thanksgiving: we have become Eucharist, one with Him. "*So whoever eats me will live because of me*" (*Jn* 6:57). We must learn with thanksgiving at Mass to become ourselves "broken bread": this is the reason why we go to Mass and receive communion.

It is extremely important to meditate on the Mass, on the Eucharist, on the need for thanksgiving after Mass. The Angel invites the little shepherd children to make reparation for the offences against the Eucharist, especially by those who should know Who they are going to receive, and yet they ignore Him culpably. They ignore Him because they do not experience the Mass and do not live it because they are thinking about having a celebration without Jesus. It is necessary to imitate the little shepherd children, to prostrate oneself and become a sacrifice with Jesus. That all starts with the Mass, with the correct way to believe in the Eucharist and in the Mass. So therefore it is about imitating Our Lady, to whom it is necessary to turn that She might teach us to experience the Mass, to make our lives a Mass, to make our lives a Thanksgiving in the Mass. In Mary we must become Eucharist for the world.

To Enter and Live In The Immaculate

So we turn to the Holy Virgin. In the Gospel of John (19:25-27) we read that the Beloved Disciple *took* the Most Holy Virgin into his life, into his inner home. In the same way in Fatima Our Lady asked to "be taken" into our lives, to enter into us, and She wants us to enter into Her Immaculate Heart.

There is a very beautiful relationship between the passage from John's Gospel and Fatima: John, the disciple who welcomes Our Lady, is a figure of the Church, and so every Christian who, to be a disciple of Jesus and to follow Him faithfully, must become a child of Mary. There is no true follower of Christ unless they are one with the Mother of Jesus: *"Here is your mother!"* (*Jn* 19:27) are the terse words addressed to the Christian.

Our Lady revealed such a beautiful secret at Fatima, that of belonging to Her through a consecration, too, to be Her property and thus become one with Her. This consecration, in turn, makes us one with Jesus. In fact there can never be opposition between Jesus and Mary. There is no need to ever fear being too "devoted" to Our Lady, believing thus one might forget or do wrong to

Jesus; that would be inconceivable and contrary to the Gospel itself. To be disciples of Jesus, above all to be faithful imitators of His Passion, Death and Resurrection, we must take Our Lady with us: it is Jesus who gives Her to us in the terrible moment of the most acute suffering of His Passion on Calvary.

The apostle John tells us that we, too, must enter into Mary, into Her Immaculate Heart, with a pure life, a holy life, with our works which must be always scented by love of God. That is only possible if they are achieved in Mary, with Mary, with the spirit of Mary. She Herself teaches us this great secret, the secret which consists in living in Her Heart, living in Her as children united indissolubly to the Mother. Thus we will live as true children of God, real Christians according to the Gospel.

The mystery of Mary Most Holy

Why do we take Mary into our home, that is, into our most intimate affairs, into our souls? Or better still, why enter into the Immaculate Heart of Mary? Why consecrate ourselves to Her? To understand the need and therefore the topicality of this request made by Our Lady of Fatima, to take refuge in Her Immaculate Heart, we must recall briefly the mystery of Mary.

Who is Our Lady? She is that purest of creatures from the hands of God, uncontaminated, inviolate, always so beautiful, never touched by even the slightest stain of sin; She is that beautiful, holy world, which belongs to God from the first instant of Her existence, the new creation, those "new heavens and new earth" (cf. *Rev* 21:1). The new Jerusalem which comes from Heaven is already present, is already a reality; She is spouse, She is a Mother, She is a Lady, She is "Our Lady", the One who was predestined from eternity to be the Mother of God and was desired to be the "Immaculate Conception" by a most high plan of divine goodness.

She, predestined Immaculate, in the fullness of time pronounced Her "*Fiat*" to God, "*may Your will be done*". That *Fiat*, Her "Yes" was an immaculate "Yes", totally pure, completely holy, with no shade of selfishness or self-sufficiency. Our Lady said "Yes" to God with Her lips because She had already pronounced that obedience with Her life, with Her total existence.

For this simple reason God gives us the Immaculate Heart of Mary. On earth She is the sole immaculate creation, is that most pure space in which we can enter and thus dwell in the "House" of God, exactly in that true and pure creation, where we can be freed from every compromise with sin, from all that offends God.

Our Lady is the dwelling-place of God with us; if we dwell in Her, if we consecrate ourselves to Her, we dwell where God dwells, where God is, because God dwells only where there is no sin, where there is purity, beauty, immaculateness. God is purity, beauty, immaculateness. We enter into this Heart, we give ourselves wholly to Our Lady and so we will be able to dwell with God. For this reason the Immaculate Heart is the "refuge" of Fatima, the alternative to the destruction of sin, to the eternal perdition of Hell.

Why not humbly ask Her, as children, to welcome us into Her Heart, to make us dwell in Her, to take us under Her protection? Only thus will we truly dwell with Jesus and with the Most Holy Trinity. With Our Lady we glorify the Most Holy Trinity, we adore the Most Holy Trinity, because It has given us this Mother and with our Mother we adore God so that in Her we might be saved eternally and thus sing the new song forever.

ONE WITH JESUS AND MARY

We have said that Fatima is the grace of being able to discover Our Lady as "refuge", in other words as "Ark of salvation", in opposition to destruction, to sin, to the general confusion. Mary

Most Holy is a gift of God for all of us, She is the Mother who leads us to God. To welcome the grace which She gives us to be able to be one with Her in consecration to Her is really important.

Two particular devotions are linked to this Marian consecration: the Miraculous Medal and the Marian Scapular, both signs which visibly want to tie us to the Immaculate. Consecration to Her, in fact, must become a moment of our eternity. For each soul who decides to carry it out, it is the moment (which no longer ends) of total belonging, without limits, without conditions to Our Lady; it is the belonging of love to Her, certain that She will make us one with God. This is Her role as Mediatrix: to make us belong wholly to God.

It often happens that we become frightened, become victims of prejudice, conceiving of Jesus as alternative to Mary and Mary almost as a rival to Jesus, in opposition to Him. So those who choose Our Lady, who are "too devoted", would distance themselves from Jesus and from His love; viceversa, whoever is truly devoted to Jesus would move away from Mary. In truth, the problem lies in an erroneous concept of the relationship which exists between Jesus and Mary Most Holy and in the final analysis in a conceptual deficiency which for some years in these parts has characterised the ecclesiastical lexicon: the disappearance of the word *analogy* (participatory likeness).

God predestined the Son and His Mother in Him as an original couple which had to recapitulate Adam and Eve and make reparation for their disobedience. There is a fundamental and original covenant between Jesus and Mary, the covenant of the eternal predestination of both and their being one – *one dear thing* – in bringing about our salvation. Therefore, between Jesus and Mary there is no rivalry, there is no opposition, but complementarity. Jesus renders Mary participant in His redemptive mystery and Mary participates in Jesus' human nature so that that mystery is realised, then offering Him Her maternal collaboration.

At Fatima Our Lady also revealed this fundamental unity between Her and Jesus: speaking to the little shepherd children, the Angel said: *"The most holy Hearts of Jesus and Mary have designs of mercy on you"*. On them, but also on all those who welcome the mystery of Fatima and discover the beauty of this Message. From then onwards, the Hearts of Jesus and Mary would always be presented together, as one Heart. The Hearts of Jesus and Mary beat as one.

On the reverse of the Miraculous Medal, too, there are two pierced Hearts: the Heart of Jesus and the Heart of Mary. It is through the Heart of Mary that we reach the Heart of Jesus; and by giving ourselves wholly to Jesus we belong truly and wholly to Our Lady. We must always be aware of this unity, of this communion. The very beautiful spirituality of Montfort asks precisely this of us: "To be Jesus through Mary and Mary through Jesus". It is a grace, then, to ask Our Lady to make us Jesus through Her and to ask Jesus to make us Mary through Him, like Our Lady. Then we will truly have achieved our Christian vocation.

We open the heart to this sublime and heavenly gift of the consecration to Her and we live according to this commitment. What does it mean in practice to live consecration to the Immaculate Heart of Mary? The commitment to observe the Ten Commandments of God – to be Mary through Jesus is certainly the start and the goal of consecration – putting them in first place; from a life morally good, true, holy, according to the will of God, will immediately derive prayer, faithful prayer and devotion above all to the Holy Rosary, a sweet bond which unites us to Heaven, a chain of grace which unites us to God.

From the observance of the Commandments and from the prayer of the Holy Rosary can only come a virtuous life, according to the measure of goodness, according to what is most perfect according to God. If we do that we will progress in the exercise of the Christian virtues and in every action we will ask ourselves: what would Our Lady have done in my place? How, in this particular case, can I be for Jesus His Mother? How can I now be for the Mother of Jesus, Jesus Himself? What would Jesus do? How would Our Lady act in this circumstance? Prayer and the virtues make us become Jesus for Mary and Mary for Jesus.

We will also understand that our concern should not be about "settling accounts", that is, in measuring what we have done for Jesus and Mary in order to then demand reward, but rather, in being one with them: to become Jesus in Mary by means of Her Immaculate Heart, in Her Heart.

By this act of giving to Her – consecration in fact is *self-giving* completely to Her – we must offer Her ourselves, what we are, our families, all we have, our inner life, our problems, our daily affairs, everything. We place everything into the hands of the Holy Virgin and everything will be transformed by Our Lady, in glorious praise of God. She will purify us from sin, will make us pure in the sight of the Son, will make us live for God, according to God, in the beauty of God. That is Mary's role, not alternative to that of Jesus, but subordinate and complementary. So we ask Her humbly to take us with Her into Her Heart and protect us in it: then we will truly live for God for eternity.

THE FLAMING SWORD

The Holy Father Benedict XVI, in his brief visit to Fatima in 2010, reminded us that the Message of Fatima is a wide open prophecy on the future of the Church and humanity. Fatima is still a current prophecy. The vision of the Angel with the sword ready to strike humanity because of its crimes must make us reflect seriously. This is the Angel of Yahweh who wants to do justice for the now intolerable sins of men and women. We are now experiencing the stage of so-called "transhumanism": human beings wanting to go beyond themselves, no longer with any identity, ignoring being a creature. Isn't this already a destructive delusion? But a maternal hand tries to stop the Angel's anger. That hand holds back the sword which is ready to strike against humanity. A voice repeats: "*Penance! Penance! Penance!*". It is the vision of the third part of the Secret, which summarises the Message of Fatima.

The little shepherd children repeated that the Lord "*was already much offended, but nobody paid any attention*". And in fact He continues to be offended, above all in the Most Holy Eucharist, by irreverent behaviour, by Christians who approach it in a state of mortal sin, but eat and drink their own condemnation (cf. *1 Cor* 11:23). Men and women seem to want to self-destruct and really no one is paying any attention. This flaming sword is there ready to strike against humanity.

The Holy Father added something else which is very important. While up until recently the enemies of the Church were outside it, today, instead, something new and at the same time disturbing is happening: the enemy is in the Church. The enemy declares himself to be a child of the Church. This enemy is growing within, while praying, adoring, and praising God. This enemy has infiltrated the Church and is living within it. Isn't it true that this sword is threatening the Church in an even more vehement way? Over those who on the one hand have made a profession of loyalty to the Church and on the other contribute to confusing souls, to scandalising them with their public behaviour and to losing them?

Sin now seems to be just a sad reality of past times, of a Church clinging to itself, which thought only about denouncing sin, invoking Hell and the condemnation of hardened sinners. For many, even pastors of the Church, sin would now seem simply a reminiscence of times which have been completely overcome, of a Church which no longer exists and which must never exist again. There is talk of "mercy", but what is meant is "emotionality", no bond, no truth. Only my "I".

In this situation, whoever participates in the Sacrifice of Jesus, anyone who goes to Fatima, but believes that sin no longer counts, does not exist, in fact is emptying Faith from within, not because Faith is founded on sin, of course, but because unfortunately this sad reality does exist. Jesus Christ, our God, has poured out His Blood to redeem every sin. To say that sin is a fantasy, an idea, a behaviour now to be overcome, means saying that Jesus, our God, has poured out His Blood for no reason. It means saying that Christianity is the religion of good intentions. This is the reason for that appeal: "*Penance! Penance! Penance!*". Intentions, no matter how beautiful, do not save.

As for the sword which looms over the third part of the secret, Cardinal Ratzinger, as Prefect of the Congregation for the Doctrine of the Faith, said: "man himself, with his inventions, has forged the flaming sword". We have forged it with our technological industry. Now the threat between countries goes straight to the concluding paragraph: nuclear war. Where is God in all of this? He has been exiled. Such selfishness! The sin of humanity removes God and places human beings "in flesh and blood" in His place. The sole remedy, therefore, is the fervent appeal: "*Penance! Penance! Penance!*" with a view to opening minds and hearts to God.

Our Lady recalls this sad reality and, at the same time, as benevolent Mother tries to stop the sword which threatens us. The sharp sword is looming over us and we do not notice it. We have distorted the principles of our Faith, we have adapted them to humanity as something which can be simply accommodated to our own needs. We want everything to be for us, to satisfy our freedom. God, too, one minute denied, one minute approved, by virtue of our successes or failures in life. By virtue of a distorted freedom is behaviour against God justified.

At the start of the 20ᵗʰ century the dictatorship of modernism was in force: there was an attempt to change the dogmatic formulae by accommodating them to the historical and temporary needs. Today, things have gone beyond that. Then, there was still belief in dogma and hence a desire to overcome it. Now, instead, it is materialised, but without any belief in it anymore. In this there has surely been some development.

For so many people sin is the mere appearance from which there is a need to liberate oneself, a sort of spectre of evil which follows us everywhere. There can be liberation from it by choosing the "fundamental option" – about which we have already spoken – in other words, remaining fundamentally orientated towards God (so one should not be sinning), even if then in concrete choices it happens that erroneous (but not sinful) choices are made. Hence disobedience of the Commandments as well as their observance becomes the same thing. To kill a child in the mother's womb or enable the child to see the light of day are the same thing. In this way human behaviour, people's responsibility before God, which is such in every act and circumstance, is emptied. That is why the Lord is very much offended. We have become more arrogant, we want to commit evil and we are proud of it, we justify it by virtue of our freedom. In the end, even God would be incapable of redeeming us from this evil, because we want our freedom. Freedom without God is against itself.

The Message of Fatima places before us this tremendous scenario: a sword which is becoming increasingly sharp due to pride, tyrannical technocracy, wants to distance us from God, to get us to believe we are already saved and redeemed. We are impoverished and we are glad to be so. What is the remedy for this abyss, so facile, so tempting and technologically advanced? Prayer and penance, requested by Our Lady which are the heart of the Gospel. When Jesus began His preaching, in fact, He said: *"Repent, and believe in the good news"* (*Mk* 1:15), because the Kingdom of God is not a matter of food and drink. To be saved and to enter into eternal Life it is necessary to change ways of thinking and living; we must put to one side our pride, our misery, our presumption before God and accept his gentle yoke, which is the yoke of humility, the yoke of recognising ourselves as sinners, of doing penance for our troubles. Only when we recognise that we are sinners before God, do we recognise our reality as limited, wretched people. Thus God enters our lives. If we humble ourselves – after all as He Himself has done – He does raise us up.

At Fatima the Lady dressed in White offers the alternative to secularisation, to this way of thinking and living, in the Church and outside it, as if God did not exist. Instead the Most Holy Virgin warns us: if we still think of acting as if God did not exist, the sword falls upon us inexorably. She will no longer hold it back. It is urgent to return to God doing penance.

We must pray to Our Lady that She might give us this awareness. The most beautiful way in which to ask Her for the grace to return to God and to do penance for our own sins consists in the recitation of the Holy Rosary. At each of Her apparitions She asks for this blessed prayer. The Rosary is truly a Crown of grace, a totality of roses of *Ave Marias* which desire to implore from the Immaculate Heart, from Her, Mediatrix of all graces, the grace necessary to live in conformity with God's Commandments.

The Holy Virgin helps us to renounce the ideology of post-modernism, which is not a theory of some enlightened people or atheist philosophers, but the prevailing ideology in the Church today: a faith sadly emptied from within, even though beautiful words with their persuasive strength are multiplying. To reject an empty faith, without God, and to welcome instead the Word of the Gospel to live as children obedient to God is the invitation of Fatima. To live as children faithful to God is the start of renewal for the world: we will make reparation for the sin of pride and we will transform the poison of disobedience into a sweet liqueur of

God's love. Thus we will become the start of the renewal for the whole Church. If the Church in itself, in its children, is holy, it will contribute to sanctifying the whole of humanity.

IN HER "FIAT"

"While he was saying this, a woman in the crowd raised her voice and said to him, 'Blessed is the womb that bore you and the breasts that nursed you!' But he said, 'Blessed rather are those who hear the word of God and obey it!'" (Lk 11:27-28.

This Word of Jesus at times appears embarrassing, almost like a re-shaping of the figure of Mary. A woman praises Our Lady: "'Blessed is the womb that bore you!", while Jesus seems to reduce the dignity of His Mother saying: "Blessed rather are those who hear the word of God and obey it!". Can that ever be true?

A protestant interpretation sees in this passage a manifestation of Jesus' scarce Marian piety and therefore of the Church's false Marian piety, since Jesus first of all seems to state that yes, Our Lady bore Him in the womb, but that does not make Her particularly exceptional – for Luther the wood of the Cross has the same dignity as Mary! – while truly "blessed" are those who listen to His Word.

Instead we find the correct interpretation of this pericope in the Fathers of the Church. In particular, Saint Augustine says that it is certainly not a re-shaping of the figure of Mary Most Holy, but rather praise which increases and shifts from the simply physical level, which is divine Motherhood, to the supernatural level, a wider Motherhood towards all the Lord's disciples. Jesus shifts praise of His Mother from the physical level to the higher level of discipleship, and that is not to ignore the greatness of the Theotókos, but uniquely to present Mary to everyone as a perfect model of discipleship and therefore the model to imitate. That would horrify Luther.

For Saint Augustine, Mary is more blessed for having listened to the Word of God and having put it into practice than for being the Mother of God. This is because it is more perfect to listen to and put into practice the Word of God than it is even to bear God in the womb. In fact Our Lady not only bore God in Her womb as mother, but above all listened and put into practice His Divine Word, fulfilling God's will in an exceptional manner. That Word which in Her became Flesh, became first truth in Her intellect, love in Her desire and then flesh in Her womb. Mary, says Saint Augustine, heard the Word of God, consented to it in Her mind, welcomed it in Her Heart, and finally conceived it in Her womb. The Word became truth in Her mind and flesh in Her womb. The Word became flesh in Her because it was generated in Her soul. Therefore Jesus is certainly praising His Mother for this exemplary motherhood which She shows to all His disciples. One cannot be a Christian while ignoring this praise of Jesus to become disciples with Mary, in Mary: in that womb which is one with Her heart, Her mind, all Her soul. The whole of Her life was at the service of the Lord.

We, too, must always begin from what is most noble, from what is most perfect: to conceive God, His Word of truth with intelligence and adhere to it. It is necessary then to welcome this Truth into our lives with love, loving it; in that way the Word of God will be flesh in our flesh, life in our lives; this Word, becoming our intelligence, our will, starts out from us ourselves, from our spirit, will then become our nourishment and we will generate it through good works. But once again that would horrify Luther.

The greatness of Our Lady and Her fundamental role in the formation of the Lord's disciples is therefore made manifest by the words of Jesus: who more than Her or better than Her has done the will of God? Who better than Her can teach us to do it? To Mary, then, we must ask that She always gives us the desire to welcome the Word of God, to protect it in our lives by meditation and to translate it into holy works; it is the love which transforms us in sacrifice and only through sacrifice is it possible to truly show our love to God. In this way His Word becomes flesh in our lives. Blessed, therefore, is Our Lady. "All generations will call me blessed" (Lk 1:48). She is the humble Handmaid who said: "Fiat, may Your will be done". She fulfilled his will, always.

If we, too, want to be "blessed", it is necessary to state our fiat to God every day, with the Fiat of Mary Most Holy. Here once again is what it means to consecrate ourselves to Our Lady: to unite our fiat to Hers and thus remain focussed on God! We must declare our "yes" in Her. Alone, with our troubles and weaknesses, we will be really incapable of fulfilling God's will each day. Belonging to Her allows saying yes to God with Her own Heart. Rightly, we, too, can be called "blessed" if we belong to Mary. That beatitude in which Jesus praises His Most Holy Mother will apply to us, too. It will resound for us like a canticle echoing the Virgin's words: "All generations will call me blessed", because I have always done God's will. In that lies refuge, salvation. Our Lady wraps us in Her "Yes" to God, that salvific "Yes", that "yes" which brought our salvation to completion. Blessed is Our Lady and blessed we will be if we recognise this beatitude of Mary! So there remains only to welcome Our Lady as Mother, to give ourselves always to Her saying to God, every day, the "yes" of our faithfulness, of our love.

"HERE IS YOUR MOTHER"

A particular passage of Saint John's Gospel constitutes the key for our Marian devotion:

> "*Meanwhile, standing near the cross of Jesus were his mother, and his mother's sister, Mary the wife of Clopas, and Mary Magdalene. When Jesus saw his mother and the disciple whom he loved standing beside her, he said to his*

mother, 'Woman, here is your son'. Then he said to the disciple, 'Here is your mother'. And from that hour the disciple took her into his own home" (*Jn* 19:25-27).

Our love for Our Lady and our giving to Her can well be called a gift of this divine revelation. In the encounter of John the Baptist, too, with Jesus, the Evangelist uses the same form to present an event of revelation; as soon as he sees the Lord, the Baptist says: "*Here is the Lamb of God who takes away the sin of the world*" (*Jn* 1:29). Similarly, on the Cross Jesus turned to His Mother and said: "*Woman, here is your son*", and to the son: "*Here is your mother*". That "here" in both cases is revelatory. On Calvary, Jesus reveals that His own Mother must also become our mother. She, who gave life to Jesus, on Calvary becomes our mother, giving life to us, too. In this way Jesus reveals the great mystery by which His Mother becomes our mother, through John, who is a figure of every disciple, of every Son of God.

Our Lady is our mother, because more than our earthly mother She has given us eternal Life, She has regenerated us as children of God on Calvary. Therefore it is a duty for us to welcome Our Lady, to take her into our lives.

We have now understood that devotion to Our Lady, and therefore consecration to Her, are not simply gestures of more or less intense piety, but rather a necessity of the Christian life. Jesus *reveals* that Our Lady is our mother: so welcome on the part of the disciple is essential.

Anyone who really wants to participate in the Sacrifice of the Cross, who wants to be reborn each time in the Blood of Jesus in the Sacrifice of Calvary, which is Holy Mass, must welcome Our Lady, live in union with Her. So it is important to ask the Holy Virgin, at each Holy Mass, to make us understand anew the words of Jesus from the Cross on high: "Son, take this Mother! Become one with Her and then you will truly and fully participate in the mystery of Redemption".

To take Her among the most intimate things

The Latin text of this pericope from John's Gospel highlights especially the peculiarity of taking Mary Most Holy with oneself. Having presented the revelation of Mary, the "Woman" – as mother of John and in him our mother – the text tells us that the disciple *"took her into his own home"*, in Latin: *"accepit eam discipulus in sua"* (*Jn* 19:27).

It is very important to note here the use of the neuter (*in sua,* which denotes that it is not about the disciple's house where Our Lady was housed, but about his "things", those material and even more those spiritual. John took Her as his property, among his most important things, among the things of his life, among all the things that he held most dear, in other words among all that constitutes John as a disciple of Jesus, all that realises his existence: his life, his soul, his inner reality, his identity as a man and as a Christian, therefore his vocation to be an apostle of Christ. Furthermore, we know that John, like the other Apostles at the Last Supper, had also been ordained a priest, and therefore took Our Lady with him into his priestly life. Everyone can see in John the prefiguration of how to be a disciple of the Lord . What is important is that the Holy Mother was received among his most important things.

Our life is a gift of God, which comes to us from the immaculate hands of Mary, through Her mediation. We are not, as is widely thought, fruit of a blind, casual evolutionism; we are not the product of a complex of atoms whose casual and confused movement produced our intelligence, our soul, our person. That would be absurd! It would be saying that from confusion and irrationality comes reason. This is false and besides impossible. Reason cannot come from irrationality. Love cannot come from chaos, from confusion, from hatred, from disorder, from evil. Intelligence comes solely from God, from the One who is Reason; love comes solely from God, from the One who is Love. At the origin of our lives there is the gift of God and this gift comes to us through the mediation of Mary.

To welcome Our Lady into our lives means recognising that this life does not come about by chance but from God. We are God's children. We have received this gift and we must guard it. Let us place it into the hands of the Most Holy Virgin.

To consecrate ourselves to Her, then, means loving life, defending life, always, at every moment and above all at the very first moment which is its beginning, that beginning which must be jealously guarded and defended. Men and women should never claim to put their dirty hands on the mystery of life, on its beginning. Consecration to Our Lady makes us defenders of life at every moment, in every situation, at all costs, because life is the greatest gift of God. Let us place our lives, which we have recognised as God's gift, into His hands. May that "*in sua*" also be for us welcome and gift of revelation.

Re-born in the womb of Mary

The episode of John who takes the Virgin with himself reveals another teaching: the Christian vocation is a gift of God through the hands of Mary. To be called to become Christians means being baptised and becoming children of God, children of the Light and no longer slaves to evil. So, the gift of Baptism, the gift of the life of grace and of eternal Life come from God through the immaculate hands of Mary.

A Church Father, Saint Leo the Great, compared the baptismal font to Mary's virginal womb, and, rightly so, because one can be re-born to new life only if one is regenerated in the same generation as Jesus, of the Son of God. Who generated Jesus? Who gave birth to Jesus? The Holy Virgin. So, to be re-born through Baptism means being re-born in Jesus; the baptismal font wishes to express that most perfect birth, which is the birth by water and by the

Spirit in the virginal womb of Mary. Therefore our Baptism is gift of Jesus *through* Mary. That water which has washed us and which has made us children is the water of grace which has been given to us through Her.

Finally, to take Our Lady with oneself, to take Her among your own most significant things, means recognising that the gift of conversion, too, comes to us from Her. We need to be converted continually, to return to the origins, to that moment when God separated us from the shadows, from sin and made us children. We confess our sins, confess that many times we have dirtied this white garment of grace. But every confession and every conversion is always a gift of the Immaculate Heart of Mary. Just as the baptismal water and the new birth in Baptism are equivalent to being born from the womb of Mary, because from there was born Jesus, so likewise to be re-born in conversion is again a re-birth from Mary's womb, through Her intercession, because through Her we have been regenerated to grace. To take Our Lady into our own lives! Or better still, to be taken by Mary's grace into Her life!

Like John, true disciple of Jesus, we, too, want to receive the Virgin Mary into our things, as our own property and to live as Her property to thank God for the gift of life, the gift of Baptism and of our conversion. It is necessary to ask Her for the grace to persevere in grace until the end: we can only obtain it by praying for it every day. Let us ask Her to be able to live always persevering in the grace of Christ and thus earning eternal Life.

Our Lady has given us the grace of knowing Jesus and understanding how important it is to do God's will: "*Your will be done*". Our Lady asks us precisely this: "Do whatever he tells you" (cf. *Jn* 2:5), do the will of my Son. Of course not only does She exhort us, but helps us through Her maternal grace to do God's will.

So we must promise Her to be faithful to the Son's Commandments, to be faithful to the Church, to be truly Christians by putting God's will into practice.

With a view to being always faithful custodians of all the graces which Our Lady wants to bestow on us, we want to ask Her to remain with us always, we want to take Her always, from today onwards, into our lives and carry Her with us at every moment.

What will be the most beautiful fruit of this consecration? To love Jesus with the Heart of Mary and to love Mary with the Heart of Jesus. The Hearts of Jesus and Mary are in fact indivisible.

Let us ask our Most Holy Mother to give us Her Heart, the Immaculate Heart, so that we can always say to God: "*May your will be done*".

Let us ask Her to always give us this authentic faith, this certain hope, this divine charity which is God. Let us say with the holy little shepherd children:

"My God, I believe.
My God, I adore.
My God, I hope.
My God, I love You.
I love You in the Immaculate Heart of Mary.
I love You with the Heart of Mary".

Under Your protection
we take refuge, Holy Mother of God,
do not despise our petitions,
but free us from all snares,
especially from the loss of the meaning of God.
Amen.

Part Four

The Secret not yet revealed

THE IMMACULATE HEART OF MARY, SECRET OF THE SECRETS OF FATIMA

The Immaculate Heart of Mary is a true compendium of the Message which the Heavenly Lady gave to the little shepherd children of Fatima from May-October 1917. The topicality and the prophecy of this Message is clearer than ever today. The request from the Lady dressed in White to Lucia, to reveal the third part of the Secret only from 1960 onwards, remains exemplary and enigmatic.

Looking at the momentous events before our eyes and the internal state of the Church – a vine devastated by the enemy: Cardinals against Cardinals and bishops against bishops, an endless field with so many deaths – we cannot but recall again the highly prophetic tone of the words of Pope Benedict XVI, spoken at Fatima in May 2010: *We would be mistaken to think that Fatima's prophetic mission is complete*. It has certainly not been completed, also because the consecration of Russia requested by Our Lady was done and repeated by Popes on different occasions, and yet Russia has spread its errors throughout the world and today the physical and moral devastation is there for all to see. What happened? Up to a few years ago it was thought that Fatima had to be consigned to the past, to the 20th century. And instead now, especially in recent years, it is returning to assert itself on the whole Church as an unheeded prophecy, as prophecy open to the future of humanity. Fatima is like a window on the world and on the Church.

Let us briefly recall the passage of Our Lady's request to consecrate Russia to Her. It was in 1929 that Our Lady, through another apparition, asked Sister Lucia to plead the cause for the consecration of Russia with the Holy Father. In precise terms Our Lady asked

> *"if you will consecrate the world to the Immaculate Heart of Mary, with a special mention for Russia, and order that*

all the Bishops of the world do the same in union with Your Holiness, to shorten the days of tribulation which He has determined to punish the nations for their crimes, through war, famine and several persecutions of the Holy Church and Your Holiness".

That is learned from the letter which Lucia wrote to Pius XII on 2 December 1940. In 1936 the Lord manifested Himself to Sister Lucia, telling her that the conversion of Russia would only happen when this nation was consecrated to the Immaculate Heart of Mary. Pius XI did not consider the request. Pope Pius XII knew about this heavenly desire and carried out the consecration in 1942, but without directly naming "Russia" for reasons of prudence. So the consecration was not carried out according to the explicit desire of Our Lady, for whom the mention of the Russian nation was decisive. Then the consecration was repeated by the Holy Father John Paul II on various occasions. The most important was the consecration in union with all the bishops of the world on 25 March 1984, but where again there was no explicit mention of Russia. To the question posed by Cardinal Bertone to Sister Lucia, if Our Lady had accepted John Paul II's consecration, the answer was yes.

But on another occasion Sister Lucia also added: *"It was done, but it was already too late"*. That is what is learned from a recent and important book, edited by the Carmelites of the monastery of Coimbra, where Sister Lucia lived and died. In the book, to which we have referred previously, extensive passages of the visionary's intimate diary (*Un caminho sob o olhar de Maria*, Edições Carmelo 2013; English translation, *A Pathway under the Gaze of Mary*, World Apostolate of Fatima 2015, p. 190) are published, including this revelation of Sister Lucia in conversation with Fr Luis Kondor, who became the postulator of the Cause of Beatification and Canonisation of the little shepherd children. This word of the visionary is reported in

Chapter X of the book, in the section about *The request for the consecration of Russia*.

This last explanation is much more plausible and explains why it did not work. The errors of materialistic atheism have been abundantly spread throughout the world. In reality, Our Lady manifested previously to Sister Lucia Her regret at the fact that the Church had not taken into serious consideration this appeal for the urgent consecration of Russia. In fact, the first response, albeit not suitable, would only come in 1942 (13 years after the formal request). Our Lord himself had already confided in Lucia in a heartfelt manner what we read in her *Memoirs*:

> *"They did not wish to heed my request! Like the King of France, they will repent and do it, but it will be late. Russia will already have spread her errors throughout the world, provoking wars, and persecutions of the Church: the Holy Father will have much to suffer".*

So is there still a need to consecrate Russia to the Immaculate Heart? Let us leave this question still open, also because it seems, from the 13 July apparition, that with the triumph of the Immaculate Heart the Holy Father would finally consecrate Russia to Mary. Let us focus instead on the need to discover a mystery which underlies everything: the secret of secrets.

A secret still hidden for many

We have almost reached the finish line of our journey in the footsteps of the Message of Fatima. Now, we will focus on the real *"Secret of Fatima"*, still hidden to many, the Secret of secrets, the *Immaculate Heart of Mary*. It is appropriate to return to this topic, even though we have looked at it in some detail before. It is so central and vital that we can try to discover again some precious pearl. The revelation of Fatima is a gift of God to our time, the

Lord who is speaking, who makes Himself present to us through His Most Holy Mother.

Retracing the itinerary of the Apparitions, we were able to understand the pedagogy of the Lord and His Mother in gradually bringing these children to understanding things that are always more profound, but always so simple and so important. And the path along which the Lord leads these children to gradually understand God's plans for them and humanity, this great path, this great crossroads, is the Immaculate Heart of Mary.

The Immaculate Heart of Mary is, so to speak, the revelation of God at Fatima. It is the Heart which guards the things of Jesus, it is the Heart which guards the truths of Faith, the Heart which exchanges places with that of God. God Himself has revealed this Heart, which is the Heart which more and better than any other is conformed to Him. It is the Heart in which only God lives, the Tabernacle of God. That is why the Lord reveals this Heart, because He abides solely in this Heart, this purest Heart: the dwelling-place of God among us. And God chooses this Heart, prepares it, shapes it as immaculate, because then He dwells in it, so that He Himself may enter into this Heart and make His dwelling, rest, and refuge there.

God takes refuge in this Heart! The Lord dwells in the immense Heavens, in His infinity, and wishing to make Himself known to us, poor creatures, He could find no other more suitable, more appropriate, place for Him, close to Him, than the Heart of His Mother, the Immaculate Heart of Mary.

So, the crossroads of Fatima, where all the Mysteries intersect, through which all roads, all words, all the revelations, the secrets, pass, is concentrated in this gift: the Immaculate Heart of Mary.

Anyone who goes to Fatima must open their hearts and welcome this Heart as gift; must, so to speak, change their heart and say: "My dear Madonna! I give You my heart, You give me Yours! I leave here my heart of stone, so hard, so deaf to God's grace, so indifferent, selfish. I leave it here, at Your feet, and You, at last, give me Your Heart".

Right from June 1917 the Lord has been telling us, by means of His Mother, that He wants to establish this devotion throughout the world, devotion to the Immaculate Heart of Mary. We have said that the Heart of Mary is the dwelling place of God among us, the place where God lives. God wants to make Himself known, to come among us, and to do so He believed that the most appropriate way to do so was precisely this Heart, to choose this Heart and reserve it for Himself. He has done so from the moment He became flesh.

But if we want to go even further back, God is eternal, the things He conceives, He conceives from eternity. Even if they happen at a specific time, God sees and conceives always and by a most simple act, which is His thought. God is His thought. Therefore, if He decided to choose this Heart in which to abide, in which to become flesh, He has chosen it, He has conceived it from eternity, and so from eternity He has seen this Heart.

As we have seen, "heart" in the Bible is not just a vital organ for human beings, it is not just a part of the body. Since the Hebrew lexicon is lacking in terms, very often there is just one term with a very broad meaning, it implies many things, has many nuances, many meanings. So, "heart" in the Bible indicates not just this vital organ of the human body, which pumps blood, but "heart" has a figurative meaning, it "*represents*" and, at the same time, indicates the inner nature of the human person, indicates the spirituality of men and women, what intimately constitutes the person.

In the Bible, "heart" indicates the thoughts of men and women; the heart is a symbol which refers to love, to thought as choice, as desire, as renunciation, as – sadly it can happen – idolatry and iniquity (cf. *Ps* 19:15; 73:7; *Sir* 37:17; *Heb* 4:12). When Israel prostitutes herself – to use a biblical word (cf. for example *Jer* 3:3ff.) – she rejects her spousal love for God, chooses other gods, idolises pagan divinities. Israel thus commits a grave sin of adultery, and adultery is conceived in the heart, just as the true love of the spouse for the bride is always conceived in the heart, not in the flesh.

In the Bible "*heart*" indicates what is part of the inner life of the human person, what constitutes the spiritual life. The same love is not conceived in the flesh, in the bones. Love, like thought, starts from the soul, starts from this inner centre of the human person, the heart.

Here our thoughts immediately turn to the "*beatitude*" of Jesus: "*Blessed are the pure in heart, for they will see God*" (*Matt* 5:8). Purity of heart is the capacity to see what is not seen. A clear heart is like a glass of pure water, like water which gushes from a high mountain, this pure heart is capable of God, because it is the human person who in his or her inner depths, renouncing idols and filth, with humility, opens themselves to God; with their intelligence, their feelings, their affections, they are capable of God, of purity, of beauty.

To talk about the "Immaculate Heart of Mary", then, means alluding to the person of Mary. When we talk about "Immaculate Heart" we want to express the mystery of Mary, Her maternal love, Her intelligence, Her affections, Her desires, Her recollections, Her memory. All that is part of the heart and issues from it. All that constitutes a person – so *in primis* their spiritual dimension – is summarised in this heart.

The Virgin Mary: a Heart which sees God

Therefore, the Immaculate Heart of Mary is the most pure Heart which sees God and becomes His Tabernacle, the Dwelling, the "*Tent*" – to use the biblical expressions – the "*Tent of God among us*". God wants to dwell in our midst and needs a refuge, a tent, and this Tent is Mary, the Immaculate Heart. God dwells in Her thoughts, in Her love, God lives in Her recollections, in Her desires, in Her aspirations, in Her concerns as Mother, in her maternal suffering: everything is shared by this presence of God in Her.

The Immaculate Heart of Mary summarises the mystery of Mary. So listen to Her at Fatima: "*God wishes to establish in the world devotion to my Immaculate Heart*", means that God wants to establish in the world devotion to Our Lady, to make us participants in the whole of the mystery of Mary, enabling us to enter into the mystery of Mary, through the door of Her Heart.

Again, to say that God wants to establish this devotion to the Immaculate Heart means that God wants to show to humanity, to the world, His one true carrier, the only place where He can be found. There are no other places. It is like saying: "Only by means of this Heart can I dwell with you, in your midst". God is spirit, God does not live in any place, because nothing can contain God. But He in His greatness was able to humble Himself. He did so when He became flesh, became man, taking our flesh in this Heart.

That is why the Lord shows the Immaculate Heart: it is His own *path* in this world. That is why, then, the Immaculate Heart is the Heart desired by God from eternity, in time, chosen and beloved so that the Son might become man, so that the Son, too, might have a Heart.

The Heart of Mary is the most ancient Heart, the original Heart. When God thinks of His Son who must become flesh, He cannot but think immediately about the way in which to become flesh, and, therefore, He thinks immediately of this Heart.

It is the most ancient Heart, but the oldest things are always the newest, most recent things: "O Beauty ever ancient, ever new", says Saint Augustine when he speaks about God in his *Confessions* (Book 10, 27.38). Mary is an ancient Heart, chosen from antiquity, from the days of old, but is a Heart which at Fatima is given to us as presence, as topicality, now. It is a Heart which the Lord has chosen always, which He wanted in time and which in this so difficult, so anguished time, gives again to men and women.

The appeal of Fatima comes at a great and important historic crossroads, at a momentous time in history. Who cannot see that our time is a great momentous situation, a turning point? A turning point when we find ourselves at a crossroads. Today more than ever we realise that we are faced with an *aut aut*: either God or destruction with a satanic sneer. John Paul II already said it when he pronounced the Act of Entrustment to the Immaculate Heart of Mary on 8 October 2000:

> *"Humanity now has instruments of unprecedented power: we can turn this world into a garden, or reduce it to a pile of rubble. We have devised the astounding capacity to intervene in the very well-springs of life: man can use this power for good, within the bounds of moral law, or he can succumb to the short-sighted pride of a science which accepts no limits, but tramples on the respect due to every human being. Today as never before in the past, humanity stands at a crossroads. And once again, O Virgin Most Holy, salvation lies fully and uniquely in Jesus, your Son".*

We think again of the nuclear bomb. We think of the fanaticism of Islamic terrorism. But, at the same time, with our technology we can make the world a garden, a place of welcome. This is the choice before us. That is why the Lord shows us this Heart. If we welcome this Heart, the world is transformed into a garden where God lives again in our midst. If, instead, we reject this Heart, the world becomes a pile of ashes, can become a sea of fire.

The Lord gives us this Heart at this time, because humanity is at a turning point, at a crossroads, at a junction which intersects with this Heart. There are no alternatives: either the Immaculate Heart, and therefore God who lives in our midst again, or destruction and Hell: "*You have seen hell where the souls of poor sinners go. To save them God wishes to establish in the world devotion to my Immaculate Heart*" Our Lady said to the little shepherd children on 13 July 1917. Either the Immaculate Heart or destruction; either the Immaculate Heart or perdition.

We enter a bit more into the Immaculate Heart of Mary and we see this Heart above all as an *Immaculate Heart*; then we see the *Sorrowful Heart*, and, finally, the *Glorified Heart* which becomes the *Eucharistic Heart of the Church*, the Heart which beats, which gives life to the Church, which has prepared for us the Eucharist, life of the Church and of the world.

THE IMMACULATE HEART: A HEART WHICH BELIEVES, HOPES AND LOVES

Let us recall the episode of the Annunciation. Our Lady receives the angelic greeting which tells Her: "You will be the Mother of the Most High". After She understood that She could preserve Her virginity promised to God, that She could preserve Her Heart immaculately – She had promised to keep it virginally, so that she might preserve God's splendour in Her (cf. *Lk* 1:34) – once She had understood what the Angel's words meant, She said: "*Fiat!* Let it be done to me according to your word".

The Heart of Mary is an Immaculate Heart: "Hail, full of grace!". It is a fullness which means not only the absence of sin, and therefore the preservation from original sin, but also and above all the fullness of grace, as gift of God, and therefore the fullness of the graces, of the divine favours, which She will then distribute as Mother to all Her children. Her immaculateness means absence of original sin and every other sin, from which stems, therefore, absence of every inclination to evil, every doubt, seduction, temptation. In Our Lady this human misery which is in us does not exist, by God's grace, because She is Immaculate.

There are no doubts about the Faith, there are no temptations, even though some people want to suggest these errors, saying that Our Lady is a "working woman", a woman like all others. This teaching is rather a "working theology", which does not have much solemnity; it has some disciples, but not many.

The Immaculate Heart is therefore a Heart in which abides the fullness of grace, absence of sin, of concupiscence, of weakness and therefore of the inclination to evil. There is the fullness of the grace of Christ, a fullness which has made Her unique. So Our Lady prepares the fullness of the Church: if She is not full of grace, She who precedes, the Church will not be holy and immaculate, but, as some suggest, sinful. It is blasphemy. The Church is not a sinner. As Saint Ambrose says it is *"immaculata ex maculati"*. But his analogy about dependence in being with the Virgin remains: if Our Lady is not completely Holy, if She does have the fullness of grace, the Church cannot be completely Holy in itself, as salvific mystery. There will only be children, a bit like us, half-measures.

Instead, the Church is completely Holy, because there is Jesus, the Head of the Church, and because there is Mary, who is the type of the Church and the model of the children, the archetypal model of the Holy Church. The Immaculate Heart is the fullness of grace, that fullness which Our Lady will then dispense as Mother to Her children, to those children who take refuge in Her Immaculate Heart. Those who take refuge in Her Heart find God's grace, that Grace which we need, because we are sinners.

The Immaculate Heart, without stain, is the Heart which believes, it is, in some way, the *faith*. Immaculate Heart means knowledge of God without hesitation, without doubts, without so many limitations which are our ignorance. Mary's faith is constant and at the same time it grows and always perfects itself more. It is not a wavering faith, like ours, fumbling in the darkness of doubts, which often makes us exclaim: "No, I no longer believe anything... But God... But this illness... If God exists why must I suffer?... If God exists why does He make that person, those innocent people suffer?"

God wants to establish in the world this devotion to the Heart of Mary, that is He wants to establish once again the Faith of Christians, if they welcome this Heart, which is the one Heart which truly believes, which does not waver, which never hesitates; it is a Heart which simply believes: "*Let it be done to me according to your word*" (*Lk* 1:38). Her *food*, like Jesus, is to do God's will (cf. *Jn* 4:34).

The Message of Fatima places us before this world of great atheism, of materialism, of indifferentism which, in fact, would come from revolution in the world. This world is not human. Against this turbid wave, this tsunami of filth, of materialism, against this wave of dirt which risks devastating the world, the Lord sets the Immaculate Heart, the Heart which has faith, in which the faith has never wavered. The Heart of Mary remains in God, remains uncompromising with faith in God. From the Annunciation to Calvary, through the Presentation of Jesus in the Temple, Our Lady experiences a progression in faith: She believes and in believing always knows more thoroughly the will of God, to the point of offering Jesus, as Co-redemptrix, on Calvary. She knows and believes more. This is the faith which is opposed to desecration.

Today we are witnessing a *desacralisation* not just of sacred things, so to speak, but also a desacralisation or desecration of natural things! The things of life, those obvious things, without which we cannot live, are brought into question. This means touching rock bottom even more! We have rejected God. We have barred Him access by a turbid wave of atheism and materialism. And now we are putting our dirty hands even on natural things, on those things which do not require faith, but which are part of us, of those people of flesh and blood which is all of us. Human beings of flesh and blood who have disowned the spirit in their bodies, now in the name of the spirit disown their bodies. We have destroyed the body and the spirit. Against all of this, the Lord, in His logic – the logic seen as stupidity by the world, of the weakness of God – to our impertinence opposes the weakness, the smallness, humility, the Heart of Our Lady.

In the immediate post-Conciliar period there were some theologians who ridiculed the requests made by Our Lady at Fatima. Some were asking, with irony, how had it been possible to oppose the Communist Revolution, so disastrous, with consecration to the Immaculate Heart of Mary. In the face of a monster, such as the Soviet Empire – today divided into so many other empires of substance – was to be placed in opposition something so small, so ridiculous! The consecration to Our Lady was being belittled. This is the wisdom of the world, of those who think that to fight you need just missiles, nuclear bombs... Then a heart attack is enough and you die. A small headache and you no longer know which button to push.

The Lord humiliates us, makes us understand how stupid we are, and makes us understand it with humble things, simple things. To oppose to the world's wisdom the folly of the Cross is the wisdom of God. The consecration to Our Lady is the wisdom of God in this stupidity of the world, the wisdom of the Cross, in the smallness of three humble little shepherd children. The Heart of Mary is the heart which also believes for us, Her children. We must reiterate it and understand it anew: whoever wants to believe in God without hesitating, without risking founding their lives on methodical doubt, assailed by so much arrogance, must have the Heart of Mary, the Heart which says: *"Fiat, may your will be done"*.

Furthermore, the Immaculate Heart is our hope. It is *hope*! The certainty of possessing what we believe, which the Lord gives us in faith, and not yet in vision, but which one day He will give us in vision and no longer in faith: the eternal homeland. Our Lady's hope is the hope of one who already possesses God, has Him in Herself, in Her Heart; God dwells in Her Heart and then He will dwell in Her womb. In this sense, Our Lady is our hope, because She gives us what we hope: eternal Life. What is eternal Life? It is Jesus, Her Son. *"And this is eternal life, that they may know you, the only true God, and Jesus Christ whom you have sent"* (*Jn* 17:3).

Anyone who truly wants to hope, without despairing, without falling into desperation, must seek refuge in the Immaculate Heart of Mary. How much anguish there is in the world, how much desperation in us, when our lives no longer have any meaning! How do you hope? How can I seek God? Where do I find God? In the Immaculate Heart of Mary.

Finally, the Immaculate Heart of Mary is a Heart which *loves*. It is *charity in action*. Faith, hope and charity in Mary. Charity is the Love of God. Charity is love which does not seek its own satisfaction, which does not seek its own egoism. It is the love which gives, which offers itself, like the Lord: *"No one has greater love than this, to lay down one's life for one's friends"* (*Jn* 15:13).

Our Lady has this charity, because, when the Lord asked Her to become His Mother, She did not let Herself be terrified by fear: "But what will happen to me. ... I am a young girl, how will I bear all these things? ... And my plans, my dreams, my ideas...". Anyone who has charity does not discuss with themselves. They say: "Lord, You will take care of it. In the meantime, I love You, then You look after things".

The Immaculate Heart is the Heart of charity, the Heart which loves God, Charity is not just doing good deeds. Everyone knows how to do good deeds, but not everyone knows how to love God, because love implies faith, and faith generates hope.

If there is not faith and hope, nor is there charity. Charity is to have faith and hope in God, and therefore to have faith in what God has said, and so to desire to love Him with all one's heart.

Through His love we do good; through His love we are charitable. There is never true charity towards one's neighbour if the nourishment of charity, which is God, is missing. Charity towards one's neighbour is not simply our actions. We can do many things, but we delude ourselves about being charitable if we think that charity is that good deed. It is not that! That is a human act! What makes charity is God's grace, which is unseen, it is its content, which is Love of God. Charity is that salt which seasons and gives flavour. If the salt of the love of God is missing our actions are insipid. The flavour of charity is love of God.

We must not understand charity in a materialistic sense, otherwise we remain material beings; we can also help those in need, but if we do not love God, that good deed remains a human act, perhaps philanthropic, perhaps selfish. How many volunteers look to themselves when helping their neighbour. How many philanthropists put themselves on the pedestal of human love so as to love themselves even more? So what is the greatest act of charity that I can do to someone? Give them 100 Euros? No. It is to give them the love of God, to give them the faith, to bring them to the faith. This is the charity we must do!

And this is something we must tell to our "*Caritas*" organisations, which think they are doing charitable things simply by welcoming foreigners. It is not enough! If we don't give the Gospel to these people, if we do not give the Truth, we delude ourselves about being charitable. Our charity becomes a "social centre". And so many "*Caritas*" centres are totally secularised, are merely humanitarian welcome centres. The Council can do this, the region can do this, the country should do it or perhaps the European Union. The Church is not a non-profit socially useful organisation or an NGO.

The Lord asks us to open the heart to true love, to His Love. And so if we give God in charity, we give everything. We give God and we have given everything. And how can we give God? If we have the Immaculate Heart of Mary. The Heart of Mary is the Heart which gives God. With the Immaculate we can and must recite every day the prayer the Angel taught the little shepherd children: *"My God, I believe, I adore, I hope and I love You! I ask pardon of You for those who do not believe, do not adore, do not hope and do not love You!"*

Sorrowful Heart

The Immaculate Heart is a Sorrowful Heart. It is Immaculate because in Mary immaculate is Her faith, hope and charity. This Heart, then, is a Sorrowful Heart because the fullness of grace which the Lord has given Her entails sacrifice for Her part.

At Fatima Our Lady asks for our sacrifices not because She likes to see us suffer, but because She had to suffer before us – sacrifice is true love – and because there is no grace without participation, without co-operation, without sacrifice.

"Sacrifice" is not an 'ecclesiastically incorrect' word. We have said it means, in reality, "to make holy" our action. If Our Lady asks the little shepherd children to help Her save souls by their sacrifice it is because She, as Mother, has made so many sacrifices for us, for our salvation and because in the divine logic only the Cross, human folly, is the salvation of humanity.

Yes we can say that that Heart is Immaculate, and therefore already blessed, because Our Lady is Immaculate. But that Immaculate Heart is Sorrowful, is pierced by pain! And do not think that our pain is equivalent to the pain of Our Lady, because Her pain is unique, it is an indescribable pain, it is the pain of Jesus. Precisely because She is Immaculate, She suffered more than everyone because the purer the heart is the more it suffers, the more sensitive it is to suffering. A heart imbued with sin is a heart which gives itself no pain, it is not a sensitive heart.

Our Lady has generated us, through Her maternal birth pains. While, in bringing Jesus to light, She had no pain, because *always Virgin* – She gave birth without pain, without birth pains, without lesions, because *always Virgin*: this is the dogmatic nucleus of the virginal birth of Our Lady – in generating us, in giving birth to us, on the other hand, Our Lady suffered at the foot of the Cross. This suffering was announced to Her right from the Presentation of Jesus in the Temple: "*And a sword will pierce your own soul, too*" (*Lk* 2:35), a sword will pierce You. Just as the Heart of Jesus is pierced on the Cross, so the Heart of Mary is pierced in Her being always with Jesus, right from that event in the Temple, the prelude to the Sacrifice of Christ. Our Lady hears from Simeon those terrible words and Saint Luke, after a while, notes: "*But Mary treasured all these words and pondered them in her heart*" (*Lk* 2:19), She nurtured them in Her Heart.

Our Lady, preserving Simeon's words and then the words of Jesus Himself: "*Did you not know that I must be about my Father's interests?*" (*Lk* 2:49), meditating on them carefully, and seeing the whole of the life of Jesus in the light of those words, united Herself to the suffering of the Son with His Heart. She prepared in Her Heart an altar of offering and of immolation to God's will. There She returned to the Father that Son She had received from Him.

The Immaculate Heart is a pierced Heart. Only those who allow themselves to be pierced by the sword of Jesus, by the sword of His Love, which asks for our co-operation, our sacrifice, is a true heart, a heart like the Immaculate Heart.

We must not say: "May grace and faith save us from all the most difficult situations in life". So many times we think that we Christians are truly so if everything goes well for us. God is with us, is present if everything goes smoothly. But this is *"predestinationism"*. We think of judging the presence of God in us by the effects of our life. We think mistakenly that God is in our lives if we are predestined to goodness, if everything goes well, if our lives are successful, if there is no suffering. Then God is with me. Otherwise, God is not with me, God is not there. This means, in truth, being Calvinist: that is, measuring God's presence by our success. This is materialism: measuring God's capacity on the basis of our capacities! It is all highly ridiculous!

The Immaculate Heart is always a heart pierced by the sword of pain. That is why Our Lady can also ask us: "Do you want to help Me? Do you really want to collaborate with me? Take refuge in My Heart. Take My Heart and learn from Me to collaborate with Jesus, learn from Me to accept suffering, to carry your cross each day. Take My Heart and you will learn to suffer with patience, to make of everything a sacrifice".

Our Lady asks precisely this from the little shepherd children: "*Make of everything you can a sacrifice and offer it to God*". She, the Co-redemptrix of humankind, teaches it to us.

Glorified Heart

Finally, the Heart of Mary, this Immaculate and Sorrowful Heart, is a Glorified Heart. From the Cross to Glory, because our lives are not just made for suffering, suffering for the sake of suffering, but suffering is for Paradise, for the glory of God, to live in the glory of the children of God. The more mine is an immaculate and sorrowful heart, that is, the more my heart participates in the suffering of God who co-redeems, so much more is it glorified, so much greater is my glory in Heaven.

The Sorrowful Heart of Mary is a Heart which co-redeems, it is the Heart which watches over us and saves us, which collaborates with Jesus in our salvation. We can be "co-redeemers" with Our Lady, with Her Immaculate Heart, offering ourselves. In so far as we have participated in the suffering of Christ and of Mary, so we will participate in their glorification, too (cf. *1 Pt* 4:13).

The Cross brings us to Paradise. The Heart of Mary saves us from ruin, saves us from perdition, because in Her God has placed His tent in our midst. She is glorified in Heaven.

After the Cross, after Her maternal suffering, after Her pain, there is glory, the glorification. Our Lady is assumed into Heaven and, as a great sign for the whole of the Church, She is assumed to Glory in Her body, too, and that means that the *whole Heart of Mary has been glorified*. Her body, too, Her Heart, all that constitutes Her person, is taken to God's side. The glorified Heart of Mary is the Heart which watches alongside the throne of God, sees our needs and intercedes for us with the Lord, Her son. It is the Heart which lives in glory, alongside God.

Being outside our time, in eternity, Our Lady sees all our needs, sees all our needs in this time, now, tomorrow, to the end of our lives, because She is not here with us, She is on high. And from on high, from this present which never ends, which is Eternity, Our Lady sees every moment, every succession of time, sees our time. It is, therefore, that of Mary, a Heart which watches over us, which is the Heart which takes care of us, which looks after me.

Just as Jesus, glorified in Heaven, exercises a heavenly Priesthood, because alive, He intercedes for us with the Father for our salvation, so Our Lady, alongside Jesus, intercedes for us, watches over us. She is like a mother who, when her son is not yet home, does nothing but watch and wait, until the son returns. So Our Lady watches over us tirelessly from on high and waits for our coming. It is the Heart which gives us God's graces.

The Sorrowful Heart is the Heart which acquires the graces; the Heart of the Co-redemptrix, which earns the graces for us through Her maternal sacrifice. The Glorified Heart is the Heart which dispenses those graces, like a rainfall which comes down from Heaven and waters our earth. The Glorified Heart of Mary is the Heart of the Mediatrix of all graces.

The Eucharistic Heart of the Church

Because glorified, this Heart is the Immaculate Heart which now guides the Church, it is the Heart of the Church. It is the Heart which is beating in the Church. The Immaculate Heart is the Eucharistic Heart of the Church. In what sense? Not in the sense that Our Lady is in the Eucharist, but, if we reflect well, the Immaculate Heart prepares the Eucharist, is the first living Tabernacle, which will give shape to our tabernacles. The tabernacle of our churches is the Heart of Mary. In this Tabernacle is Jesus. In Her Heart we find Jesus, because Jesus dwells there.

The Eucharistic Heart is the Heart of Mary, because through Her flesh and Her blood, Her love, Her maternal care prepares the Eucharist. Jesus is made flesh in Her, takes His flesh from Her to then offer Himself in sacrifice. Without human nature, God cannot offer a sacrifice, cannot immolate Himself, cannot die. God assumes human nature, a body, from Her, to offer a sacrifice. Our Lady prepares this sacrifice, prepares the gift of Jesus, which remains in the sacramental form of the Sacrifice, which is the Eucharist. The Lord humiliates Himself in a fragment of bread! So the Heart of Mary is the Heart which prepares the Eucharist, which kneads the flesh of that Sacrifice.

If the Heart of Our Lady prepares the Eucharist, "kneads" it with Her flesh and Her Blood, then Our Lady prepares the mysteries of the Church and among the mysteries there excels without doubt the mystery of the Eucharist, *Mysterium mysteriorum Dei.*

Again, if the Eucharist is the heart of the Church – the Church lives the Eucharist, the Church is made by the Eucharist – then, consequently, the *Heart of Mary is also the Heart of the Church.*

Let us go over it again. If the Eucharist is the Heart of the Church, because the Eucharist makes the Church, the Church exists because there is the Eucharist, because Jesus gave Himself and left Himself as a Memorial, we are Church because there is the Eucharist, there is the Body of Jesus; we are His Body because we have the Eucharist, we eat His Body, the true Body which makes the mystical Body. The mystical Body of Jesus is the Church and the real Body of Jesus makes the Church. Therefore, the Eucharist is the Heart of the Church.

Our Lady, the Holy Virgin, is the Heart of Jesus, it is the Heart which has prepared this Eucharist; Our Lady is the Heart which always prepares the Church, which moulds the Church, because the Eucharist is prepared by Her, therefore the Church is prepared by Her, is born *in Her*. This does not mean that Our Lady – in very poor terms – is greater than the Eucharist, but it is to underline simply that a mother is always at the origin of her son, the mother gives life to her son, who, even though he may be an independent person, nevertheless remains bound to her.

Our Lady, the Mother of Jesus, is always beside our Tabernacles, in fact, She is the Heart-Tabernacle which guards Jesus, is that Heart which always adores Jesus, alongside the Tabernacle, and which beats for love of Jesus. From all that derives the fact that there is no true participation in the Eucharist, in the Holy Mass, in Eucharistic Adoration, without the Immaculate Heart of Mary. We cannot truly live the Eucharist, also ourselves become Eucharist, Sacrifice, without the Immaculate Heart of Mary. If Our Lady prepares this Sacrifice with Her sacrificial Motherhood, She will prepare all of us to be "sacrifice", transform us in the Eucharist. We, too, become in Her and through Her, Eucharist, sacrifice pleasing to God.

The Christian life is precisely this: to become Eucharist. Jesus has given us this Sacrament which is the greatest of all. And the whole Church lives this mystery, there are no other purposes. The

Church is not an association of people who desire power, money and careers. Many times it seems that in the end there is only this, but this is not the goal. The Church lives for the Eucharist and Our Lady prepares all Her children to become Eucharist themselves.

PREPARING THE TRIUMPH OF THE IMMACULATE HEART OF MARY

And so we come to the Triumph of the Immaculate Heart of Mary promised to Lucia. We all desire this "triumph", but perhaps we are a bit too triumphalist, we think of things in a triumphalist manner.

What is this *Triumph of the Immaculate Heart of Mary*? We all want to know: has it started? When does it start? When does it end? And what happens? And before...? They are legitimate questions, but let us get to the point. When will this triumph really happen? When this Most Holy Heart of Mary becomes our heart, when we have this Heart, when we belong to Her. And therefore, if the Virgin Mary becomes the Heart of all of us, She gradually becomes the Heart of a great part of the Church. And then we hope that She becomes the Heart of the whole of the Church, so that everyone belongs to this Heart. And if everyone is consecrated to this Heart, then it truly triumphs, because thus *the Heart of Mary becomes the Heart of all of us, becomes the Heart of the Church* and thus finally the world can be saved, the world can be brought to that space where God dwells, can draw close to God.

The Heart of Mary is the salvific space of God in this world. Without the Immaculate Heart of Mary, God does not save us: there is no other way for Him to come into our midst and to remain with us to bring us with Him.

Without the Immaculate Heart of Mary, God does not work, God does not triumph. God triumphs when the Heart of His Mother triumphs, because in this way we are saved and the world, through us, can be saved. So we can understand how beautiful it would be if the Church, starting from the Pastors, would take into serious consideration this request from Our Lady. The Popes have done so a number of times. Now what are the bishops waiting for to consecrate themselves to Our Lady and to consecrate their dioceses to Our Lady? What are parish priests waiting for to consecrate themselves to Our Lady and to consecrate their parishes to Our Lady? What are Christian families waiting for to consecrate themselves and to consecrate their children? Everyone must become Mary's property! Surely all of us can make ourselves apostles to our bishops, our parish priests, our friends for the consecration to Our Lady.

And thus we arrive at the essence of the Message of Fatima: the Immaculate Heart of Mary which asks us to consecrate ourselves to Her. God Himself wants to establish this consecration to the Immaculate through devotion to Her Heart. We consecrate ourselves to Our Lady when we give ourselves to Her unconditionally, free from every bond or slavery of sin. When we say: "My dear Madonna! I give myself to You, I give You my heart; You give me Yours!". Consecration is an exchange of hearts. It is like saying: "Here at Fatima I leave my old self, with so many problems, and perhaps many sins, and I want to re-clothe myself as a new person". I want to re-clothe myself in Christ.

And who is really new? Who is always new, all in Christ? Our Lady, the Immaculate Heart of Mary, only Her. This is the consecration we must do: "My dear Madonna, I give you all of myself, what I am, my capacities, my intelligence, my heart, my life, my sins, I give you all that I am, You give me everything that is You. Give me Your Heart, so that I may be truly of God, Give me Your Jesus".

Let us not make any fuss, let us not raise fruitless and useless problems by saying: "Well! *Consecrate yourself* to Our Lady... A contradiction with Baptism. It is enough to be consecrated to God. Better to *entrust yourself* to Our Lady", with the risk of thus toning down not just the gesture but the mystery itself. These are really human trifles in the face of this great and urgent request from the Immaculate Heart of Mary.

Our Lady said to Lucia: "*My Immaculate Heart will be your refuge*". "*Refuge!*" It means that you must enter into this Heart; do not take refuge in Her if you do not enter therein with your life! And how do you enter there? It is not enough to entrust yourself to Mary, like entrusting money to a bank, money which nevertheless remains your own. You enter there if you *consecrate* yourself, if you become Mary's property. God consecrates us in Mary. Precisely this "being under the protection", "to find refuge" in Mary, belonging to Her, is expressed by one of the most ancient Marian prayers:

> "*We fly to thy protection, O holy Mother of God, despise not our petitions in our necessities, but deliver us always from all dangers, O glorious and blessed Virgin*" (3rd century).

Will I just want to entrust myself to Our Lady? And say: "My dear Madonna, I give you something, but woe betide You if You touch my things! The money is mine, life is mine, woe betide You if You touch me! No suffering... nothing... You stay there, I am here, and as soon as I want, I'll take my money back, and I'll ask You for everything You haven't given me!" This is entrustment. Do we want this?

"*Consecration*", on the other hand, is Christian perfection, concerning the things of God, without making human distinctions: "I give You myself, the whole of myself, and I will never take myself back. *Totus tuus Maria ego sum et omnia mea tua sunt*".

This is charity in action, like the Immaculate Heart of Mary: giving without wanting to receive, self-offering without demanding anything in exchange. This is true love! True love is gift of self. The Immaculate Heart of Mary makes us love like the Lord. Today, we, too, are at a Marialogical crossroads: either consecration or entrustment. Let us leave entrusting to the banks. We want greater things!

Let us end by asking Our Lady to make us understand this secret of Fatima, the secret of secrets: *Her Immaculate Heart.* This is the secret which Our Lady gives to each of us. Blessed are those who, in the secret of their hearts, enter into this spiritual space, the "*room*" Jesus speaks about: "*But whenever you pray, go into your room and shut the door and pray to your Father who is in secret*" (*Matt* 6:6). And what is this inner room? The most beautiful room in God's palace is the Heart of Mary.

Let us ask Our Lady that we may be able to understand this grace, this opportunity which She gives to us all. Thus we can truly preserve the words of Jesus in a genuine manner, without falseness, without dilution. Let us preserve the genuine words of Jesus, let us conserve the living Memory of Jesus, which is precisely Our Lady, who preserves Jesus and therefore conserves for the whole Church, for all of us, the words of the Son.

Whoever does Mary's will, in a most excellent manner, in the most perfect way, does the will of God. The Immaculate Heart of Mary is that Heart which always and only does the will of God. And this is the will of God manifested at Fatima for our time: *to consecrate oneself to the Immaculate Heart of Mary.*

About The Author

Fr Serafino M. Lanzetta is currently resident in the diocese of Portsmouth (UK), where he is priest-in-charge at St. Mary's, Gosport.

In 2004 he gained the license in Theology at University of the Holy Cross in Rome and in 2006 the doctorate in Theology at the same University, with the thesis *Il Sacerdozio di Maria nella teologia cattolica del XX secolo. Analisi storico-teologica* (Casa Mariana Editrice, 2006).

In 2014 Fr Lanzetta gained the habilitation in Theology with a specialization in Ecclesiology at the Theology Faculty of Lugano (Switzerland), under the direction of Prof. Dr. Manfred Hauke. His thesis was *Il Vaticano II, un concilio pastorale. Ermeneutica delle dottrine conciliari* (Cantagalli, 2014); English tr. *Vatican II a Pastoral Council. Hermeneutics of Council Doctrines* (Gracewing, 2016). He is lecturer in Dogmatic Theology at the same Theological Faculty and collaborates with the School of the Annunciation at Buckfast Abbey – England. Fr Lanzetta is also assistant editor of the Theological Journal *Fides Catholica* and has collaborated with *L'Osservatore Romano*.

Printed in Great Britain
by Amazon

26121499R00130